PARK CITY

PARK CITY

A KNOXVILLE NEIGHBORHOOD HISTORY

MARGERY WEBER BENSEY

THE History PRESS

Published by The History Press
Charleston, SC 29403
www.historypress.net

First published 2012

Manufactured in the United States

ISBN 978.1.60949.406.3

Library of Congress CIP data applied for.

Notice: The information in this book is true and complete to the best of our knowledge. It is offered without guarantee on the part of the author or The History Press. The author and The History Press disclaim all liability in connection with the use of this book.

CONTENTS

ACKNOWLEDGEMENTS

Thanks to all the talented writers, artists and historians who have inspired me, worked with me, provided information and shared knowledge. Thanks to my great family and friends who have gone on field trips with me, traveled back in time with me and cheered me on in creating this book. Thanks especially to my editor, who learned of my work and invited me to write this book, and to the staff who combine efforts to produce book after book and at last now mine. Thanks to those who bought this book and care about who or what was here before we were. We are kindred spirits! Thanks to all who contribute to historic research and preservation, making our earth a better place.

Chapter 1
RESEARCHING PARK CITY

How I Came to Write This Book

Twenty years after my husband and I found our historic house, when the house was one hundred years old, I was invited to write this book.

We bought the house together, researched its history together and started restoring and decorating at the rate of a room a year. We raised our son here, had gatherings of family and friends and put our house on the home tour circuit. We started meeting and talking with members of the family who had built our house, inviting them for visits and hearing their stories. Together, my husband and I started exploring and researching the area around our house. We located and identified Barber-designed houses throughout Park City and explored and maintained the antebellum Shieldstown Cemetery near our home.

Throughout those twenty years, I printed our research in community newsletters, posted it on various websites and presented it at local readings. A piece I wrote about finding and falling in love with our house was published by the University of Tennessee Press in the state bicentennial anthology, *HomeWorks: A Book of Tennessee Writers*, and again by Greyhound Books in *Knoxville Christmas 2008.* Photographs of our house appeared in Arcadia Publishing's *Images of America: Park City*. And of course, I was at work on a book of my own.

And through one of those many printings, postings, presentations and publications, my acquisitions editor at The History Press learned of my work and invited me to write this book. And here it is, a condensed version of the book I had begun to write twenty years before.

But it all started with finding one house in which to live with my family and loving them and the house for twenty years.

THE WINTER OF BLACKBERRY CORNER

We found Blackberry Corner on the first day of winter. The morning had been silvery cold, the sky filled with white clouds and gray-white air, as though it were going to snow, the trees tall brushes against the sky. It was an ordinary tall white two-story house, somewhat in need of paint, with a row of white columns along the curve of the veranda, sitting on a muddy bank up over the street amid a cluster of bare plum trees. In the backyard was a small pond filled with black water and sodden dark leaves. I was already bending to peer down into the dark waters. My hand brushed the leaves at the edge of the concrete. "Look, here's an inscription," I said, "*November 14, 1944*. That's when the people who lived here built the pond."

That would be the Etters, said the realtor, Martha. The Lanes, who lived there next, had filled in the pond with earth and planted a rose garden in it. But the Stallmans had dug it back out so that it was a lily pond again and had kept it stocked with goldfish. We stood over the pond, imagining its past and its possibilities, picturing waterlilies in summertime. And then Martha unlocked the back door and took us inside the house.

The house had been built in 1909, on a double lot in Elmwood Park. There had been eight fireplaces that burned coal. The chimneys had long since toppled, tall and narrow, made of brown brick and eroding mortar, like the chimneys on the Creamers' house down the street, and the bricks had been hauled away.

The house, with its old-fashioned kitchen, had been built by the Blacks. Mr. Black had been a conductor on the Southern Railroad. Every night, he would have come in through the kitchen door. Every day, Mrs. Black would have gone to the market or sent their son Claude, unless she had an icebox. Then the iceman would have come to put ice in it. Near where the icebox might have stood was a vintage refrigerator with rounded corners, and on the opposite wall a large white enamel double sink. Both of them looked old enough to have belonged to the Etters, or even the Blacks.

We next walked into the dining room and gazed around us at the tall china cupboard with glass doors and the heavy linen chest with curlicues carved on the front, both of the same dark wood, coated in layers of blackened shellac, both built into the walls. The linen chest, which fit under the foyer stairs, had six drawers, two feet wide and three feet deep. The china cabinet stood as high as the ceiling. I opened the doors and looked inside at the wavy glass panes and the shelves for plates and dishes.

In the foyer, the woodwork was splendid. Shining oak wainscoting paneled the walls, and French doors opened onto a little parlor with an ornate corner mantelpiece. Beside a massive front door set with thick beveled glass rose the curving dark bannisters and balustrades of the stairway. The Blacks' daughter Annie had been married at home; she had come sweeping down the stairs on her wedding day and had moved into the little gabled house next-door. Which was Annie's room? Was it there at the top of the stairs? The stairway walls loomed in light and shadow, rising twenty feet to the ceiling above. As I climbed the stairs to the second story, looking down at the tremendous woodwork below, I thought, "This house has been waiting for me to live in it and preserve it." I was ready to buy the house.

We had expected to buy a bungalow, covered in vines, awash with hedges and flowers. We had planned names we could give it and colors we could paint it: Periwinkle Cottage, Raspberry Cottage, Blackberry Cottage. We could plant periwinkles or raspberries or blackberries if there weren't any already growing in the garden. But now, instead of a bungalow, we had a high house on a corner overlooking all of Knoxville. I surveyed the front yard with its muddy banks covered in ivy and what looked like a profusion of mimosa and mulberries on the corner where the two streets met. I said, "We'll call it Blackberry Corner."

Our families wanted to know how we were going to manage, living in a cavernous ten-room house with peeling wallpaper, drafty doorways and a twenty-foot hallway down the center of each floor. *We* wanted to know who had lived there before, what they were like and what the neighborhood had been like. I was sure that Annie had had the room at the top of the stairs above the parlor, with its mirrored corner fireplace and flowered wallpaper. I chose it for my own sitting room and not long afterward began stripping the eight layers of old wallpaper down to the pinkish-brownish flowers that would have been Annie's when the house was new. Michael chose the sunny back room overlooking the lily pond. I could tell that he was blissful, planning for waterlilies and goldfish.

We lost no time in meeting our neighbors and in finding out more about who had lived in our house and in our neighborhood. Blackberry Corner had been built in the Elmwood Park neighborhood in what was then the town of Park City, northeast of Knoxville. In the little house across the street lived Mr. Sexton. Where Mr. Sexton's house stood had been a pasture when Mr. Sexton was a boy, with cows and horses grazing, and East Fifth Avenue had been a dirt road, built out as far as Lake Ottossee in 1886, with a stop on the trolley line at Elmwood Station. There had been only two other houses, the Rosses' on the opposite corner and the Creamers' down the street. Mr. Sexton had grown up on the next street over, but he knew the Blacks, Claude who was his boyhood friend, and Annie, who was older—Mrs. Brannum, he called her.

Mrs. Rymer lived in the brown brick apartment house behind Blackberry Corner. Before the apartment house was built, the land it was on had been woods all along Magnolia Avenue, right up to the edge of Blackberry Corner. Annie Brannum's seven children used to play in the woods, as Annie herself had probably done. They all had grown up in the house next-door, with a little gabled room for every child or two. The Brannums had lived there for sixty years; a young man who lived next-door in the gabled house had bought it from Annie herself.

We researched our house and its families at the courthouse, tracing the deeds back through the Stallmans, Longs, Lanes, Etters and Blacks, and at the library, poring through city directories, thick books listing name after name, street after street, year after year, with occasional advertisements for mantelpieces or coal services. The Etters had lived there the longest, twenty-four years; they had bought the house from the Blacks' daughters. Mr. Black had left two daughters the house in his will, dated 1926. They were career girls, listed in the directory pages as Miss Helen and Miss

Frances, stenographers for the Bell Telephone Company. They had kept the house rented out all through the 1930s, like a boardinghouse, while they lived next-door with the Brannums. Another daughter, Pansy, was listed in the directories as well.

Mr. Black's will was in the courthouse among the house deeds. We read it, our heads together in the shadowy downtown daylight, the new owners-to-be of Blackberry Corner, years after it had been written and the designations therein had come to pass. Claude had been left out of the will almost entirely. We wondered why. What was the story behind it? Claude got five dollars, and his sisters got the property. Claude worked for the Louisville and Nashville Railroad, a railroad man like his father, following in his father's footsteps. Was Claude well-to-do in 1926, wanting for nothing, or was Mr. Black displeased with him? We rather thought the latter. There was a Claude Black listed in the Knoxville telephone book. That might be him. But we couldn't call and ask.

I went back to the library time and time again that week to research the history of the house. Hunching over thick books until my shoulders ached, I yearned for a way to go back in time and see Blackberry Corner eighty winters before with its eight little coal grates lit for the winter, its inhabitants moving through the shadowy rooms. If only I could find old brown photographs of the Black family and Blackberry Corner. What had the house looked like? How had the sisters dressed?

In the library, I read about life in the Knoxville area in 1915. One could not buy ready-made clothing back then; everything one wore would have to be sewn by hand. People either made their own clothes or called in a seamstress to make them. Good ventilation was important because of the coal fumes; social workers visited poor people who lived along First Creek and did not know enough to open their windows. Coal dust left streaks of black on peoples' wallpaper, and workers with huge gum erasers were called in to clean it off.

In the library's special collections were Sanborn fire insurance maps of Park City. The earliest one was from 1917. On it were diagrams of all the houses in Park City, including the Elmwood Park neighborhood. I was excited, taking the map with eager hands and peering at the tiny inked outlines of houses, porches, walkways and outbuildings. I found Blackberry Corner on the corner of East Fifth Avenue and Holly Street, and behind the house, outlines of what the librarian said were probably an outhouse and a stable.

So there had been an outhouse, where the apple tree stood now, and a stable along the alley, "a one-and-a-half-story wooden building with a composition roof." The old pebbly concrete foundation of the stable was still there at Blackberry Corner; we had seen it: two raised garden beds with concrete edgings and a driveway in between, where the places for two horses and a carriage had been.

Neighboring houses and outbuildings were inked in delicate black lines as well. In 1917, East Fifth Avenue and Magnolia Avenue were scattered with occasional houses amid the woods and meadows. Volumes of the old city directory supplied more details about Elmwood Park around the turn of the century.

Down East Fifth Avenue from Blackberry Corner was the Creamers' tall and narrow house with stained-glass windows, built in 1892. Mr. Creamer had been a manager for the Western Union Telegraph Company. His house had a porch across the front, a shed in the backyard and a fifty-foot chicken coop along the alley. The Creamers' house was still standing, and inhabited, but the chicken coop was long gone and the shed was a heap of toppling boards.

Across Holly Street from Blackberry Corner, the Rosses' house had been built in 1894. The fire insurance map showed a huge structure with wings, turrets and a circular veranda. The Rosses had a lumber company on Willow Avenue in Park City and a business in Knoxville, Ross and McMillan Box Manufacturers, where the whole family worked, even Mrs. Ross, who kept the books.

Mrs. Ross lived in that magnificent house the rest of her life. After Mr. Ross died, Mrs. Ross took in boarders. After Mrs. Ross died, the house stood empty and was torn down in 1958. The Rosses' stone wall was still there, and their stone steps, and their shade trees, but Michael and I were moving to Elmwood Park years too late to live near the magnificent old turreted house. I felt disappointed at having missed it. How sad it was that so much of our history and culture was being deleted from the surface of our city.

Outside the library window, dark was falling. I had spent Saturday afternoon leaning over the volumes, following names through decades.

My shoulders were stiff, and my eyes saw spots. It was dinnertime, and the library was closing. I pulled my wraps around me and made my way up the hill in the blustery evening to the gray house where Michael lived on Highland Avenue. There we would celebrate the New Year.

The well-lit house welcomed me as I reached the top of the hill. In one window was a Norway spruce hung with strings of cranberries, a silver star at the top. In another window was Thomasina the cat, silhouetted against the light in the hallway behind her, observing the comings and goings of the neighborhood. The freezing air seared my lungs. I wrapped my muffler about my face and breathed through the cold wool and ran up on the porch.

The downstairs was full of housemates and friends. I went in and stood in the kitchen while Michael dipped hot cider into my mug. Sitting at the big kitchen table with our cider mugs in front of us, we drew the rooms of our house on a napkin, trying to remember the nooks and closets and how the halls narrowed and jogged at the back of the house. We had made an offer on the house, and it had been accepted; we were beginning to refinish the wood, paint the walls and plan the gardens.

Blackberry Corner, 2009. *Photo by Margery W. Bensey.*

It was the new year and a time for new beginnings, but we were going back in time. It was 1989, but we would live in a 1909 house, read about life in 1909 and learn more about the family who lived in our house in 1909. Those were our inspirations and our resolutions as we looked forward to planning our wedding, moving into our house and raising our children. And, we vowed, if we could, we would live to be a hundred, keep the house in the family and keep our own history alive at Blackberry Corner.

A PORTRAIT OF BLACKBERRY CORNER

We bought Blackberry Corner on March 24, 1989, and immediately began restoring our historic house. We first landscaped the garden and decorated the dining room, then held our pink-and-white garden wedding at the house on May 20, 1989. We had music and poetry in the garden, and then our family and friends were served pink cake and pink punch in our rose-and-blue dining room.

We spent the next two decades restoring and decorating the interior at the rate of a room a year, and we repaired and painted the exterior at the rate of a side a year. We also avidly researched Blackberry Corner and its environs for the first decade that we lived there. I was employed as a writer and editor at a nearby university and often spent after-hours time researching our home in the library and online.

And ever since we bought Blackberry Corner in 1989, we wondered what life was like in our house when it was built in 1909. We had an inkling in the winter when we walked down our drafty, unheated twenty-foot central hallways or waited for hot water to flow up three stories from the old coal cellar to the second-floor tub. We could imagine in summer when breezes wafted through the twenty-six tall windows or we lay in the hammock in the shade of the wisteria.

After we had been living there for around five or ten years, I was able to establish contact with various descendants of the Black family, and I was told stories by one family member, given a genealogy by another and sent pictures by a third.

The old sepia-toned photographs of the family, taken not at Blackberry Corner, but at their Pearl Place house in Oakwood shortly before they moved, were sent by Annie's granddaughter Susan Cooke Peck. They were pictured in their garden in front of a bower of catalpa trees and in their parlor surrounded by Victorian walnut and wicker: Mr. and Mrs. Black with their five children, Annie, Pansy, Claude, Frances and Helen.

In the first portrait, taken outdoors in front of a grove of catalpas, Annie stood with her parasol, wisps of curls escaping brown hair pulled back from her face, Pansy beside her, frowning a little in the sun. Both were wearing dresses with bloused waists, puffed sleeves and lace frills at the elbows. Claude was just a little boy, wearing a striped sailor suit that he already seemed to have gotten dirty. Frances was a tiny girl in a white dress and black ankle-strap shoes, held in the arms of her mother; Helen may not have been born yet. The children's father seemed to have been the photographer.

In the next portrait, we could catch glimpses of their parlor furnishings. An ornate Victorian piano was draped with a fringed velvet scarf. The chairs were dark wood and light wicker. At the window was lace drapery

The Black family in their garden, 1906. *Photo courtesy of Susan Cooke Peck.*

The Black family in their parlor, 1909. *Photo courtesy of Susan Cooke Peck.*

and on the wall was a collage of what appeared to be photographs and visiting cards. I wondered where that might be today.

A dark carved parlor dresser with a tilted mirror stood in the corner, reflecting the profiles of family members: daughters Annie, a young lady with her hair done in puffs, and Pansy, a young girl in a sailor dress with her hair pulled back in a big bow. Claude, a young boy in a dark suit, stood to the side. Seated in their parents' laps were little Frances and baby Helen.

Also in the picture were two relatives who lived with the family: Isadora Elisabeth Day's brother William Day and his wife, Mary Rose Burnett. I would later find in my research that Dora and Will were members of a large Day family long established in the neighborhood and that Mary Rose was a member of a large Burnett family who had lived in the area as well. Both families had been established in the neighborhood since the 1880s, when the hills and roads were part of a farm village known as Shieldstown.

We were also sent portraits of the lady of our house, Isadora Elisabeth Day, and her husband, William Green Burleson Black, who were married in Knoxville on July 11, 1892, at the ages of nineteen and twenty. The pair of portraits appear to be from this era, their years at Blackberry

Corner two decades after their wedding, when Dora and Green, as they were called, had reached middle age. Dora seemed serious and gentle, looking a little away from the camera, her brown hair piled softly atop her head, her high-necked white shirtwaist trimmed in dark stripes. Green was dapper in a dark suit and mustache, meeting the camera head-on. These portraits, which probably hung in the front parlor then, are back in the front parlor now.

On September 6, 1909, Dora and Green purchased the property at Blackberry Corner. They built the house later in the year and moved in with their five children. The census records from April 3, 1910, show them already living there, so it was likely that the house was built that autumn 1909, before winter weather set in. Later, we met more family members and were given a portrait of the house the year it was built. And that was the picture I had most wanted to see.

Blackberry Corner, 1909. *Photo courtesy of David Correll.*

A Visit to Blackberry Corner

When we had been living at Blackberry Corner for about fifteen years, we had a visit from the Blacks themselves. At about two o'clock on a Monday afternoon, Annie's eldest daughter, Dorothy Brannum Correll, arrived at Blackberry Corner on the arm of her niece Patricia Fowler Watson, one of Annie's granddaughters. I saw them coming up the veranda steps and went out to greet them. The gracious lady replied, "Please call me Aunt Dot." It was a momentous occasion. Dot had lived at Blackberry Corner as a child but hadn't been back in years. Pat had never been inside at all.

As we walked into the foyer, Aunt Dot said, "We always had our telephone right there on the south wall." And there on the baseboard opposite the door, ninety years later, a little old-fashioned phone jack was still screwed. The lines had still been there when we moved in—miles of wires stapled to the baseboards and woodwork, running down hallway and up the stairway. We removed all of them before we refinished the oak woodwork and pine flooring. We had always called our foyer the Plumtree Room for the pink-blooming plum trees outside, the plum-pink wedding decorations on the stairway and the plum-pink wicker with which we furnished the room.

"And this was our parlor," said Aunt Dot, gesturing. She remembered pocket doors sliding out of the walls where our French doors are now. In the corner was a tall oak mantelpiece with a mirror and pillars that had been there ever since the Blacks built the house. We had seen their furnishings in pictures: the piano with a fringed velvet scarf, the parlor dresser with a tilted mirror, chairs of dark wood and light wicker and white lace curtains at the windows. Our furnishings were cherry, and the room looked out over two weeping cherries at our entrance, so we called it our Cherrytree Room.

The back parlor of Blackberry Corner, with its shelves of books, was our library. Because of its hunting and fishing motifs and linen draperies with quail, it was dubbed the Quailbird Room. One could imagine it as the Blacks' library, too, with the parents and children gathered around the hearth with books. But in Dot's memory, it was her grandparents' bedroom, where Dora and Green Black slept. The extended family, aunts and uncles, adult children and grandchildren, had occupied the upstairs rooms; as many as seventeen people may have lived in our house at one time—where only three of us lived in the 1990s and 2000s, with our cats. Our library has a little greenhouse nook with a window, stained glass and plants, the Quailbirds' Nest. But Dot remembered the little windowed room as her grandparents' clothes closet.

Across the hall was the dining room. Aunt Dot remembered the tall built-in china cabinet that went from the floor almost all the way up to the nine-and-a-half-foot ceilings. The Blacks had a huge dark dining table, said Aunt Dot, which seated twelve, with great heavy carved legs. A great many people lived in the house, the extended families were always coming for dinner, and Green Black brought friends from the railroad home for poker at the dining table. Outside the dining room door to the veranda, he sat on the porch swing, which was where we have our porch swing, and spit tobacco juice over the edge of that nice, white veranda. Dora did not like it, especially if he missed. We painted the dining room blue, with a paper border of apple blossoms in russet and rose, in view of an old apple tree in the garden, and called it our Appletree Room.

We moved on to the adjoining kitchen. We had excavated layers of historic linoleum to expose the original old worn pine kitchen floorboards, painted brown in the era of the Blacks, but now sanded and finished to a golden shine. We painted the old pine wainscot blue—over the layers of other colors—and called the kitchen the Bluejay Room because of the flutter of blue jays in the backyard. Where we have our stove, the Blacks had theirs, a wood-burning stove connected to a brick chimney, and we could see a burned depression in a pine floorboard where someone dropped an ember. Where we have our 1930s porcelain sink, the Blacks had theirs, an older one, and we could see water damage in the darkened pine floorboards around it. The icebox was on the back porch, Aunt Dot remembered. One put a sign in the west kitchen window, and the iceman saw it from the street and stopped. A hundred-pound block of ice would last a day or two.

Outside the back door had been a woodland of trees, mostly maples, with our big old maple and gnarled old apple right where they were back then. We sat in the kitchen, looked out the window and reminisced. Out by the alley was the stable and later the Blacks' garage, where Green Black parked his 1920s Willis Knight touring car, a big car that his daughter Frances sometimes drove. Frances, nicknamed Red, had red hair, and a temper to go with it. Over the garage were servants' quarters, but the Blacks had not had any servants. In the side yard was a huge vegetable garden.

At the top of the stairs is the upstairs foyer, a little mezzanine with balustrades on two sides. There is just room for a rattan daybed under a tall window overlooking the mountains, with built-in bookshelves on either end. The Blacks, too, had a little sitting area in the upstairs foyer, with a table and sofa and chairs. Here the children had played for hours, and once a child smashed a china doll's face and another child had been cut. We call this foyer our Forsythia Room, painted forsythia yellow, papered in blue stripes and hung with my great-grandmother's blue-and-yellow quilt. Outside the window, forsythia blooms in winter.

Family legend had it that the front bedroom belonged to Annie, the eldest daughter. The day I heard it from Annie's granddaughter Pat, I felt as though I had always known it, just as the day we finished papering the room, I heard from Annie's granddaughter Sue for the first time. It's hard to know what Annie's own wallpaper had looked like; the bottom layer had faded to a light brown, with blue birds and flowers outlined in a darker brown. A later layer was light brown with silver stripes. Today the room is papered in a Victorian rose red and leaf green with a lavender border, and we call it the Lavender Room. It's my room for reading and writing, and it doubles as a guest room.

After Annie's marriage, the little pentagonal front room went to other siblings, second daughter Pansy, and then son Claude. "It was Claude's," remembered Aunt Dot. Claude was the middle child of the family, the only brother, in his teens and twenties when Dot lived there. "He kept his guns over the fireplace," said Dot. We stared at the rose-and-green paper over the corner mantel where a favorite childhood painting of mine now hangs. It was hard to imagine Claude Black's rifles mounted there.

Annie took the larger, sunnier room down the hall for herself, her husband and their babies. Anna Elisabeth Black and David Harrison Brannum were married on October 30, 1912, and lived at Blackberry Corner for the next thirteen years. Their apartment was the sunny, breezy back bedroom, our sunroom—my husband's sitting room and sometimes a guest room. He painted it a warm peach, decorated it in an Oriental style and called it the Waterlily Room, as it overlooked the lily pond, blooming summers with yellow waterlilies.

Dot could remember the Brannums having no other room. "The babies just slept with the parents." I imagined my brother's whole family, with their six children, living in my husband's back sitting room. But back then, a double bed on either side of the room would be standard, the fireplace in between. A baby and toddler in one bed with the parents, and four little girls in the other. The fireplace burned coal or wood, Dot remembered. Once the rocking chair and a quilt caught fire.

We went to the west bedroom next. It was once an upstairs sitting room, then guest room, then nursery and playroom for our son Kiernan. This room also had once been the Black children's room—Pansy, Frances and Helen. After Pansy's marriage, Frances and Helen moved across the hall to the small, dark east bedroom, leaving Pansy this larger, sunnier room for her little family. Pansy Annalee Black and J. Frederick Tauscher were married on November 27, 1914, and lived at Blackberry Corner, as everyone else seemed to. They had three sons, William, Robert and David, and eventually left Knoxville for Bristol.

On the east side of the house is a pentagonal bedroom with a corner fireplace, the master bedroom, the Rosebud Room. My ballet dancer husband decorated the room in a romantic ballet pink and white, our wedding colors. The ornate fireplace, with its mirrors and pillars, rises up in the corner like a white wedding cake. Next to the mantel is Kiernan's white spindled crib, converted to a settee, with a pink-rose-mint-and-blue baby quilt made by my childhood friend Kathryn Demlow. The room was always a children's room, Dot remembered, first Claude's, then Helen and Red's.

It was there in the Rosebud Room that "The Angel Story" took place. Dora was taken ill with tuberculosis in her forties. Her eldest daughter, Anna, was called on to care for her. Dora was brought upstairs to the Rosebud Room, where it was quieter. As Anna sat by her mother's side, an angel appeared in the window and spoke to Annie: "Don't be afraid, I'm not a ghost, I'm an angel; and I'm not here for you, I'm here for your mother, Dora." That night, Dora died. It was November 19, 1919.

Annie and Harry stayed on at Blackberry Corner to look after the family for the next six years. With six daughters ranging in age from infancy to eleven, it was time for the Brannums to move into their own house. They built a bungalow-style house next-door in 1925, which we call Brannum Bungalow, and their youngest child, a boy, was born after the move. Harry ran the Park City Grocery nearby on Sixth Avenue; it is said that Annie grew every kind of flower imaginable.

Green Black was only fifty-seven years old but not in good health when he died in 1928. He left Blackberry Corner to Red and Helen, who lived next-door at Brannum Bungalow and rented Blackberry Corner to roomers. After that, three more families owned it over the next six decades, before we bought it and began to delve into the history of the house, its families, their neighbors, the surrounding farms and towns and even the earliest settlements back in the 1700s.

Chapter 2

EARLY SETTLEMENTS

Two hundred years ago, early Knox County settlers with land holdings in the area that became known as Park City included landowner Alexander McMillan (1749–1837); Robert Houston (1765–1834), sheriff, justice, senator and secretary of state; and Moses White (1775–1830), son of Knoxville's founder, James White. McMillan, Houston and James White were veterans of the American Revolution who had served in the Battle of King's Mountain and received land for their service as part of the North Carolina Land Grab Act. They were among the first white settlers in Knox County, arriving in 1783 with several others to select property in east Knox County. McMillan, Houston and White all chose or later purchased land in the area that became known as Park City.

Alexander McMillan of Lake Park Springs

Alexander McMillan was born in County Derry, Ireland, in 1749, the son of Mary Rebecca Eldridge and Alexander McMillan. He immigrated to America in 1775, where he had relatives in Virginia, and married his first cousin Margaret Martha McMillan in Augusta County in 1778, the year she was sixteen and he twenty-nine. Margaret McMillan was born in 1762, the eldest of ten children of Mary Leeper and William McMillan.

She and her husband also had ten children, born between about 1780 and 1800: John, Mary, Esther, Evelina, James, Sarah, Elisabeth, William, Andrew and Alexander.

McMillan fought in the Battle of King's Mountain, for which he received the land where his family settled. McMillan received nine hundred acres in property grants in east Knox County between 1785 and 1791 and also purchased more than twenty thousand acres in the Forks of the River area, making him one of the largest landholders in Knox County. The McMillan land extended from his homesite in the Wooddale area as far east as land that was to become Chilhowee Park and the Lake Park Springs subdivsion of Park City.

Around 1787, McMillan constructed a house that still stands at 7703 Strawberry Plains Pike near Wooddale, east Knox County. In those days, the pike was known as the New Market Road, and a nearby landmark was the Armstrong Ferry, about four miles away, operated by Moses Armstrong, remembered today by its place name Armstrong Ferry Road. The ten McMillan children grew up at the Wooddale house, where their

Gazebo, Chilhowee Park, on land owned by early Park City settler Alexander McMillan. *Photo by Margery W. Bensey.*

father lived for fifty years, from the time he built the house in 1787 until his death in 1837. Most of the children were born there.

Some sources state the family lived in Strawberry Plains, a small town east of Wooddale over the Jefferson County line, whose post office serves a number of hamlets and villages in east Knox County to this day, along Strawberry Plains Pike and elsewhere. But there is no record of his family holding land in Strawberry Plains.

Some sources say the family lived at McMillan Station, a small town north of Wooddale across the Holston River that bears their family name. Later, from the 1820s to the 1900s, several of Margaret and Alexander McMillan's sons and their descendants did live at McMillan Station in northeast Knox County. John, James and Andrew raised families there.

James McMillan, second son of Alexander and Margaret McMillan, was born in 1793 and grew up to marry the daughter of a prominent Park City–area family: Alice Houston. Her parents were Margaret Davis and Robert A. Houston, who owned an adjoining farm just west of the McMillan land and likely built the brick mansion still standing on old Rutledge Pike, possibly the oldest house in Park City.

Alice and James lived across the Holston River at McMillan Station in northeast Knox County in a house no longer standing, likely from the time of their 1818 marriage until 1842, when James bought a 140-acre tract on Cedar Lane in the Fountain City area. They built a log cabin near a large spring on Cedar Lane, and he kept a journal from 1825 through 1866 in which he recorded day-to-day life on his farm among family and friends.

Margaret Amanda McMillan, who married a prominent Park City area developer, was a granddaughter of Margaret and Alexander McMillan and daughter of their younger son Andrew McMillan and his wife, Mary Littleford. Margaret Amanda was likely raised at McMillan Station in northeast Knox County but lived in the Park City area after her 1852 marriage. She married John Howard Shields of Sevier County when she was twenty-two and he was twenty-five. They owned an 1854 house on Howard Street in Shieldstown, an antebellum village named for them, around which Park City later developed. Their ten children, born between 1852 and 1873, were Ella, Eliza, Samuel, Mary, Alexander, Margaret, Lawrence, Anna, William and Destovin.

Edward Epps McMillan, also prominent in Park City's history, was a great-grandson of Margaret and Alexander McMillan and grandson of their eldest son, John McMillan, and his wife, Jane Meek. The son of John Alexander McMillan and Elisabeth Epps, he was raised at McMillan Station in northest Knox County, near Meek, the old name for Mascot, likely settled by his grandmother's family. In 1882, at the age of thirty-two, he married Belle Clinton Welcker, twenty-two, a daughter of Nancy Park White and Albert Gallatin Welcker of Knoxville, and a cousin of the author's great-grandfather. Their children were Maggie Belle, Edward John and Helen, born between 1884 and 1892.

McMillan had worked in area textile mills from the age of twenty and, in 1900, cofounded Knoxville Knitting Mills, also known as Standard Knitting Mills, at the western edge of Park City, the first southern manufacturer of men's heavy ribbed cotton underwear. He was president of the mill, a major employer of Park City residents, from 1900 until his death in 1932, upon which his son Edward John McMillan served as president from 1932 until 1956. E.J. McMillan had prepared for his career by studying engineering at the University of Tennessee and graduating from the Philadelphia Textile School. He married Mamie Henegar, daughter of Mary Alexander McMillan and Edward Henegar of 1007 Circle Park. They raised three daughters at 1726 Melrose Place near the university, on which land now stands the historic Melrose residence hall.

Fernando Beaman of Beaman Lake

The Lake Park Springs section of the McMillan land in the Park City area stayed in the McMillan family for almost a century, but in 1875, the Park City holdings were put up for sale. On December 31, 1875, Fernando Cortez Beaman purchased the Alexander McMillan property in the vicinity of today's Chilhowee Park and Lake Park Springs subdivision.

Beaman and his wife, Mary Jane, from New York, had seven children. He fought in the Civil War, settled in Tennessee after the war ended and taught school in Jefferson, Sevier and Knox Counties. Upon buying the land, Beaman decided to retire from teaching and become a dairy farmer. The family lived in an old log cabin on grassy land near natural springs, which became pasture and pond for their dairy cows.

To earn a better living, Beaman returned to teaching and became a professor at Tennessee Wesleyan in Athens, leaving his wife and seven children running the dairy farm.

Then, to make more money, Beaman converted the dairy farm to the Beaman Lake resort, damming spring branches to form Beaman Lake for public swimming, boating and picnicking. When Knoxville's mule-powered streetcar system was converted to electric power in 1889, Beaman arranged to have a line extended to Beaman Lake.

He also sold off the land for the Lake Park Springs residential subdivision and, to make life in the suburbs feasible, provided electric trolley service there as well.

Two of the Beamans' children had interests in the growth of Park City. Clarence further developed the Beaman Lake resort into Chilhowee Park and brought the Appalachian Conservation Exposition to Park City in 1910 and 1911. Ruth married Jacob Aston and produced a son, Arthur Aston, who developed Park City further, building apartments and businesses.

Clarence Beaman of Chilhowee Park

Clarence Beaman married Cora Goddard and had six children: Clarence, Elizabeth (Libby), Jean, Alvin, Margaret (Margie) and Charlotte (Chickie). The family summered at Beaman Lake, where Clarence grew up, but lived in the Lake Park Springs subdivision developed on Beaman family land, first on East Fifth Avenue at the corner of Castle Street and then in a Barber-designed house at 3041 Magnolia Avenue, neither of which is standing. Today, the whole north side of the 3000 block of houses is gone.

Clarence Beaman developed Chilhowee Park into a popular resort with caves, mineral springs and the fourteen-acre spring-fed lake, now called Lake Ottossee. For the Appalachian Conservation Exposition in 1910, he built a bandstand, dance pavilion, riding stables, a swimming area and exhibition buildings. He created an amusement park with a bowling alley, Ferris wheel, merry-go-round, penny arcade, roller coaster and skating rink. Today the park is a pleasant area with green hills and curved walkways around the lake, open to the public. The Tennessee Valley Agricultural and Industrial Fair is held there each September, with amusement park attractions and agricultural and domestic exhibitions.

THE ASTONS, 1520 MAGNOLIA

Arthur Fernando Aston, son of Ruth Beaman and Jacob Aston and grandson of Mary Jane and Fernando Cortez Beaman, built three brick 1920s apartment buildings in Lake Park Springs, all of which are still standing: the Lakewood Apartments at 2730 Magnolia, the Shenandoah Apartments at 2724 Magnolia and the Aston Apartments at 2736 Magnolia Avenue.

Aston lived in Park City with his wife, Clara Nelle Burnette, and their children Arthur, Barbara and David, first at Aston Apartments and then in a white clapboard house at 1520 Magnolia Avenue in Elmwood Park. This house, built in 1886 on Moses White's land, was formerly home to his descendants Juliet Park and Andrew Park White and then home to Martha and Andrew Jackson Queener, cousins of the author.

The Astons ran a paint store out of the Whites' old carriage house. David Aston ran the paint business, AAAA Paint and Supply Company, with his father. Daughter Barbara Aston Wash was for many years a reporter for the *Knoxville News-Sentinel* and its "People and Parties" columnist.

The Astons were still living at 1520 Magnolia in 1955, but not long after that, their home became the Bellevue Hotel and then the Blue Star Tourist Home. The house is no longer standing today, though its stone wall still surrounds the lot.

ROBERT HOUSTON OF COLD SPRINGS FARM

Robert Houston—sheriff, justice, senator and secretary of state—was an early landowner in the central section of the area that would become Park City. He was raised in Abbeville, South Carolina, then came to Knox County as a young man to visit relatives and stayed for the rest of his life. The son of John Houston and Alice Armstrong and grandson of Alice

Calhoun and Robert Armstrong, he accompanied his mother on a visit to a branch of the Armstrong family who were living in Knox County.

The area was then the Territory South of the River Ohio; Knoxville was established in 1791, Knox County in 1792 and Tennessee in 1796. Houston was commissioned the first sheriff of the county by Governor William Blount in June 1792, opened the first County Court in John Stone's Tavern in Knoxville in January 1793 and then helped defend the area from an Indian attack at Cavet's Station in September 1793.

In 1794, Houston married Margaret Davis, and they were the parents of six children: Alice, Amelia, Melinda, Rutelia, Horace and James, born between about 1795 and 1810. The family lived on Cold Springs Farm, located between McMillan land to the east and White land to the west. A hundred years later, Cold Springs Farm was developed as the Cold Springs subdivision, bounded by Woodbine, Tarleton, Cherry and Olive Streets; these were the boundaries of Cold Springs Farm in 1900 and perhaps also in 1800. The brick mansion and stone spring houses of Cold Springs Farm, attributed by some to the Houston years, still

Cold Springs farmhouse on land owned by early Park City settler Robert Houston. *Photo by Kiernan W. Bensey.*

stand at 2639 Rutledge Pike, later renamed Dr. Martin Luther King Jr. Boulevard, in Park City.

Although the age of the Cold Springs Farm estate house is not known, it is the oldest known house in Park City and likely one of the oldest in the county. Houston probably began farming the land and building his house and outbuildings during the 1790s and early 1800s. The property stayed in the family throughout his lifetime. Houston was in public service from 1893 through 1828, serving not only as sheriff but also as Knox County trustee, tax assessor and justice of the peace. He was state senator during 1805–1807, representing Knox, Roane and Anderson Counties, and secretary of state during 1807–1811.

In 1818, the Houstons' daughter Alice married her neighbor James McMillan, son of Margaret and Alexander McMillan, who owned the adjoining farm to the east of the Houstons—though the Alexander McMillan house at 7703 Strawberry Plains Pike in Wooddale was several miles away from the Cold Springs house.

Amelia Houston married her cousin Drury Payne Armstrong in 1823, who in the 1830s and 1840s owned much of the land along Kingston Pike west of downtown Knoxville. Their daughter Elizabeth Armstrong also married into the neighboring McMillan family—her husband was James P. McMillan.

Melinda Houston married George Anderson McNutt, son of George McNutt, emigrant from Ireland, whose older sister Isabella McNutt had married the Houstons' neighbor Moses White a generation ago and owned the adjoining farm to the east of the Houstons.

Rutelia Houston married James Isbell. Their daughter Alice Isbell married her cousin William Park Armstrong. The futures of her brothers Horace Houston and James Houston are not known to this author.

JOSEPH MABRY OF COLD SPRINGS FARM

Joseph Alexander Mabry Jr. bought Cold Springs Farm some time after Robert Houston's 1834 death, likely by 1840, and may have added to the former house or built the current house. The Mabrys lived on the farm in the 1840s and 1850s, on what was then part of Rutledge Pike. Joseph Mabry and his wife, Laura Evelyn Churchwell, were the parents of fourteen children, twelve of whom are remembered as George, Joseph, Evelyn, William, Clarence, Charlton, Blanche, Lawrence, Herbert, Percy, Lillian and Churchwell. Only six lived to maturity.

Joseph Mabry was the son of Laura Scott Hare and Joseph Alexander Mabry Sr. of the Concord area of west Knox County. He was educated in the Knox County public schools and Holston College, as was his brother, George Washington Mabry, farmer, justice and legislator, who married Jeannette Hume and owned three thousand acres near Mabry-Hood Road. The sisters in the family were Calpernia, Margaret and Mary. Mary married H.T. Dick; Margaret married William G. Swan. Laura Churchwell was the daughter of Rebecca Evelyn Montgomery and George W. Churchwell, of the Oakwood area of north Knox County.

In 1858, Mabry built another house at 1711 Dandridge Pike, today a museum, where the family lived. Cold Springs Farm was kept in the family as a summer home, with its cool breezes, shade trees, cold springs and stone springhouses. Mabry was a downtown merchant, railroad entrepreneur and the largest landowner in the area, with sixty-one thousand acres in 1860.

During the Civil War, Mabry offered his ridge-top house and grounds to whichever side was in power and received the courtesy title General Mabry for his efforts. He and his family survived the war only to be involved in several shootings, fatal to Mabry and two sons.

After 1900, the Cold Springs farm was subdivided into a residential area, and the Cold Springs spur of Rutledge Pike changed names. The rambling brown brick farmhouse was known for over a century as the Mount Rest Home for elderly ladies. Outlying land was sold to developers, and the Cold Springs subdivision was established. The Mabrys' lives are documented at the Mabry-Hazen Museum, their former home, at 1711 Dandridge Avenue.

Moses Lusby of Still Pond

The Mabrys were good friends with another area family, the Lusbys, until tragedy struck.

According to Lusby researcher Darlene Huey, the Lusbys were from the Forks of the River area, the confluence of the French Broad and

Holston. The family patriarch, an earlier Moses Lusby, had a farm there, where soldiers mustered for the War of 1812. Their daughter, Lucinda Lusby, married William Bell, and their three sons—James Bell, Moses H. Bell and Joseph Strong Bell—fought in the Civil War. It is unclear whether or not this Bell family was related to Joseph Bell who had a farm in the the Shieldstown area of Park City area around 1810–1838.

Two respected Lusby brothers, immortalized in their obituaries, settled in the Shieldstown area: James P. Lusby, married to Mahala Harris, was born in 1819, died before 1880 and was buried in the Lusby-Burnett family Cemetery in Shieldstown; and Moses H. Lusby, married to Sophia Moore, was born in 1825, died in 1882 and was buried in the Shieldstown Cemetery. In between the two brothers were six sisters. Most of the Lusbys were living around Bertrand Street and Ramsey Ferry Road in the 1880s—James's daughters Lavinia and Amanda and son John, and Moses's sons and daughters Donald, Christopher, Georgiana, John Moses, Sarah and Mary.

The Lusbys were pillars of the Shieldstown community, related to the Burnett, Compton, Day, Eaton, Frye, Jones, Stephens and Woods families of the 1880s. Their obituaries in Robert McGinnis's *Historic Cemeteries of Old Knoxville* offer the highest praise for their characters. Mahala and James Lusby's granddaughter Mary Rose Burnett and her husband, William Day, lived with William's sister Isadora Day Black and her husband the year they built Blackberry Corner, the author's home. Mary and Will Day appear with Dora and Green Black in their 1909 family portrait, in the introduction to this book.

Sophia and Moses Lusby began married life in Asbury at Forks-of-the-River in east Knox County, then moved to the Shieldstown area with their ten children: William, Donald, Scott, Christopher, John, Georgiana, Lucinda, Susanna, Sarah and Mary. The Lusbys were neighbors of the Mabrys, living and farming near Mabry Street or Mabry Hill, but by the 1880s, Lusby progeny had houses up and down Bertrand Street in the Poplar Springs section of Shieldstown. They farmed the outlying land or worked as brick masons and paperhangers.

Moses Lusby had a pond on his Shieldstown land and, according to his great-great-great-grandson Christopher Gardner, had a moonshine still in the pond, shared with his brother-in-law John Claiborne. The still and pond stayed in the Lusby family for decades, maintained by Moses's son Winfield Scott Lusby, then his grandson James C. Lusby and then his great-grandson Roy Lusby. But the pond dried up, and the still was exposed. It was spied by a cousin, who passed down the family legend, reported by Roy's grandson Chris. It seems likely that the pond with the still was near Bertrand Street where Moses Lusby and his descendants made their homes.

Sophia and Moses Lusby's second son, Donald C. Lusby, lived on Ramsey Ferry Road near Bertrand Street, Poplar Springs, in the 1870s and 1880s. A constable and bricklayer, Don married his first wife, Sarah Burnett, in 1865 when she was twenty-one and he was sixteen, and he was married to his second wife, Elisabeth Lusby, by 1880, when she was thirty-four and he was thirty-two. In 1880, Don was a District 2 constable, and his son Willie, fourteen, lived with him and worked alongside him as a brick maker. Willie also was apprenticed to a saddler, likely Henry Day, the second husband of his mother, Sarah Burnett, whom she married in 1877. Henry Day was the older brother of Isadora Day Black, who lived in the author's home.

Don's first wife, Willie's mother, Sarah Miranda Burnett, was born in about 1844, fifth daughter of Elizabeth Sherretz and Blackburn Howell Burnett, who lived at Mill Shoals south of the Holston River in southeast Knox County. Sarah was the tenth of eleven children born between about 1821 and 1846: Joseph, Lucinda, James, Zachariah, Benjamin, William, Suzanna, George, Letitia, Sarah and Marion Preston. Some of those names became well known in Shieldstown.

In 1858, Sarah's father had bought land in Shieldstown from John Howard Shields, and her family moved to the north side of Craig Street, west of McMillan (Cruze), near Bertrand, today's 1900 block of Magnolia Avenue. The family lived in the Craig Street house until 1876 before they moved to Mabry Street, east of Patton. In 1888, Sarah's brother Benjamin Burnett sold land fronting Craig Street for widening the street, which then was renamed Magnolia.

Sarah Burnett Lusby Day died in 1881 when Willie was fifteen. Then on Christmas Eve that year, Willie's father, Don Lusby, and his buddy Will Mabry went out for an afternoon of sporting events, cockfighting and horse racing, then stopped at a tavern for a drink. The day ended with Don shooting Will dead in the street.

The Mabry Lusby Feud

According to Lusby family members, author Mark Twain and the newspapers and trial records of the day, the Lusbys and Mabrys were friends until the shooting. Moses H. Lusby's deceased wife was buried on Joseph A. Mabry's land, and their sons Don Lusby and Will Mabry often went on outings together.

A previous incident had occurred at Madam Maggie Day's establishment in Shieldstown, apparently a saloon-bordello combination, as such venues sometimes were in those days. As constable for the district, Don had barred Will from the premises for rowdy behavior.

Despite this, Don and Will remained friends, stated Huey. They had been to a cockfight at Wade's Brickyard in North Knoxville earlier in the day and then raced their horses back into town for a stop at Snodderly's bar.

Will tried to buy the constable a drink, which Don declined. Will felt insulted, and a debate ensued, escalating into a bar fight. Will smashed a plate over the constable's head; the constable reached for his pistol; Will ran for the door and out into the street, chased by the constable, who shot twice. Will dropped on Vine Street thirty feet from Gay. The constable and bystanders then sought to get him home to Mabry Hill but stopped at a house halfway there, where Will died.

A preliminary hearing was held the following day, Christmas, with Dr. Sam Boyd stating that the two shots had lodged in Will's neck and side.

At his trial the following August, the constable was found not guilty of first-degree murder and released on bond, and a mistrial was declared. Don and and his father, Moses H. Lusby, were then shot dead in the courthouse, with only a few people in the room: Joseph A. Mabry Sr., Joseph Jr., the sheriff, the clerk and a couple others.

There were no convictions. Joseph Sr. and Joe Jr. went to trial in October and were acquitted of the murder of Moses and Don—only days before they were killed in a Gay Street shootout with banker Thomas O'Connor.

Moses H. Lusby was buried in Shieldstown Cemetery with an attractive Victorian gravestone. His son Don's grave is thought to be nearby, but if marked, the stone has not survived. A large maple tree grew over the graves and then fell in a storm about 125 years later. The tree was cut and cleared by neighborhood residents, including the author, owner of Blackberry Corner, where Don Lusby's first wife's niece and her husband once lived.

The August shooting left Willie Lusby, fifteen, an orphan. He had now lost both his parents and grandparents during the 1880–1882 period. His paternal grandmother, Sophia Moore Lusby, and his maternal grandfather, Blackburn Howell Burnett, had both died before 1880, and his maternal grandmother, Elizabeth Sherretz Burnett, had left the district to live with her grandson William Burnett and died not long after that. Willie's mother, Sarah Burnett Lusby Day, died in 1881.

Willie could have continued to make his home with his stepmother Elisabeth Lusby, with Lusby family members nearby, or he might have gone to live with some of them, continuing as a brick maker or driver. He only lived to be eighteen, his short life ending in early 1885. He too may have been buried in Shieldstown Cemetery with his father and grandfather or perhaps next to his mother in the small Burnett family cemetery.

Moses White of White's Creek

Moses White, son of Knoxville's founder, James White, owned land in western Park City and begat a number of Park City residents. His was the land on which Caswell Park was built, known for years as White's Pasture, and the land along First Creek, once known as White's Creek.

Born in 1775, he was the second son of Mary Lawson and General James White, named for two previous Moses Whites, his paternal grandfather and great-grandfather. He was the third of seven children born between about 1770 and 1785: Margaret, Hugh, Moses, Andrew, Mary, Cynthia and Melinda.

During the American Revolution, Moses White's father was captain of the North Carolina Militia, received a land grant for his service and spent part of 1883 traveling down the Holston River with others to choose the land where his family would settle.

In 1785, the year Moses was ten, his father helped organize the State of Franklin; participated in the General Assembly and Constitutional

James White Fort, 1786, childhood home of early Park City settler Moses White. *Photo by Margery W. Bensey.*

Convention in Greeneville, Greene County, Tennessee; and moved with his family to Riverdale in east Knox County, Tennessee, settling on the north side of the French Broad River.

The next year, 1786, when Moses was eleven, his family joined several other families on the west side of a creek known today as First Creek. The creek was then called White's Creek, and on its banks James White and his family cleared land and built another cabin. Today that site is between Central and State Streets. The cabin and its stockades have been moved to another site on Hill Avenue, where it is open to the public as a museum, the James White Fort.

The little settlement along White's creek was called White's Fort, but in 1791, when Moses was sixteen, the town of Knoxville was laid out, named for General Henry Knox, and in 1792, Knox County was created from Hawkins and Greene Counties. James White was appointed lieutenant-colonel commandant.

In 1794, Blount College, named in honor of the territorial governor, was established on land donated by James White, one of the trustees of the college. Classes met in a two-story frame building downtown on

Gay Street, between Clinch and Church, where the Tennessee Theater was later built.

By 1798, Moses White was married, a father and farming the land on the east side of White's Creek, his property in the Elmwood Park and Poplar Springs sections of Park City. His land likely extended from today's Bell Street along First Creek east to Olive and from Woodbine south to Bethel. The location of the family home is unknown, though several descendants made their homes on this land in later years. Moses White married Isabella McNutt and had thirteen children between 1798 and 1823: Josiah, Hugh Alexander McNutt, James, George McNutt, Isabella, Mary, Jane, Samuel, Cynthia, Moses, Melinda, Catherine and Thomas.

Moses's wife, Isabella, the mother of these children, was one of twelve herself, born over a forty-year period to four mothers: Margaret, Susannah, Isabella, Virginia, Jane, William, Rebecca, Martha, James, Asenath, Mary and George. Their father was George McNutt from County Donegal, Ireland. He married Mary McNutt in 1758 in Rockbridge County, Virginia, when he was seventeen; Isabella Callison, mother of Isabella, for whom she was named, in 1779 in Augusta County, Virginia, when he was thirty-eight; Katherine Kain, in 1792 in Knox County, Tennessee, when he was fifty-one; and Virginia Anderson, in 1797 in Knox County, Tennessee, when he was fifty-six.

In 1807, Moses White donated some of his land in the Poplar Springs area to East Tennessee College, to be merged with Blount College, which his father had helped found a decade before. Poplar Springs may have been a place name in use at the time Moses White had land there; by the 1850s, it was a residential subdivision in Shieldstown, incorporated as Park City after 1900. Professor T.C. Karns, MA, described the college plan in *Contributions to American Educational History.*

> *Blount College proposed to be absorbed by the new institution for East Tennessee. Thereupon, the legislature incorporated East Tennessee College by act of October 26, 1807, and located it within 2 miles of Knoxville on 10 acres of land donated by Moses White. The spot was known as Rocky or Poplar Spring, and is now in the Shieldstown addition to Knoxville. The franchise and property of Blount College were then transferred to the new school.*

The original Poplar Springs subdivision developed by John Shields was located along present-day Magnolia, Islington and Linden Avenues between Bertrand and Keller Streets, defining a possible location for the donated land. However, the entire Shields-Blang subdivision area has been referred to as Poplar Springs, bounded by East Fifth Avenue on the north, Bethel Avenue on the south, Olive Street on the east and Bertrand Street on the west. The ten-acre campus could have been located anywhere within this area and beyond.

However, East Tennessee College was never built in Poplar Springs. After years of donations and negotiotions, a hillside location was purchased west of Knoxville and buildings constructed, the institution opening as East Tennessee University, where it has remained since, "The Hill" on the site of the present University of Tennessee.

George McNutt White, fourth son of Isabella and Moses, raised in rural Park City, grew up to serve as mayor of Knoxville, sheriff of Knox County and circuit court judge. He married Sophia Moody Park in 1827, and they lived in her family home, the historic Park House still standing on the corner of Cumberland and Walnut downtown. There they raised twelve children: Nancy, Moses, Naomi, Isabella, Margaret, James, George, Hugh, Amanda, Andrew, Carrick and Moody.

Three married sons of Sophia Moody Park and George McNutt White made their homes in the Elmwood Park section of Park City from the 1880s through the early 1900s: Juliet Park and Andrew Park White; Harriet Walker and James Park White; and Mary Martin and George McNutt White Jr. Their second cousin Hugh Lawson McClung Jr. and his wife, Ella Gibbins, had a home in Poplar Springs at that time. Hugh was a grandson of Moses White's sister Melinda and her husband, Charles McClung.

THE WHITES, 1520 MAGNOLIA AVENUE, ELMWOOD PARK

In 1900, Juliet Park and her husband, Andrew Park White, a dentist and realtor, were living at 1520 Magnolia Avenue, Elmwood Park, on the corner of Myrtle Street. First cousins who married, the couple had two daughters, Isabel and Juliet. Some of Juliet Park White's recipes are included in the *Knoxville Cookbook 1900*, such as oysters, cranberries and lemon meringue pie. Juliet's mother, Phoebe Alexander Park, and daughter Juliet White Metcalfe also contributed recipes to the cookbook, as did Nancy Scott, who cooked for the family. Juliet Park White was the daughter of the Reverend James Park, minister of First Presbyterian Church, and grew up with nine brothers and sisters at the historic Park House, still standing on the corner of Cumberland and Walnut in downtown Knoxville. Andrew Park White, nephew of the Reverend James Park, was a son of the Honorable George McNutt White Sr., mayor of Knoxville, sheriff of Knox County and circuit court judge. Andrew and Juliet were the grandchildren of Isabella McNutt and Moses White, early settlers of Park City, and the great-grandchildren of Mary Lawson and James White, Knoxville's founder.

The Whites, 1311 East Fifth Avenue, Elmwood Park

Harriet Walker and her husband, James Park White, lived at 1311 East Fifth Avenue, Elmwood Park, on the corner of Jessamine Street. White's Creek, later known as First Creek, wound through their backyard. The Whites had four children: Lucy, Walker, George and James. James Park White's brother George McNutt White Jr. also lived at 1311 East Fifth Avenue, with his wife, Mary Martin White. Mary and Harriet both had recipes in the *Knoxville Cookbook 1900*. The White brothers were sons of the Honorable George McNutt White Sr., mayor of Knoxville, sheriff of Knox County and circuit court judge. They were the grandsons of Isabella McNutt and Moses White, early settlers of Park City, and the great-grandchildren of Mary Lawson and James White, Knoxville's founder. Today the Whites' lawn is home to a fleet of Knoxville Area Transit buses.

The McClungs, 2118 Bell Avenue (Jackson, McCalla), Poplar Springs

Some descendants of Moses White's older sister, Margaret, also lived in the Park City area. She married Charles McClung of Pennsylvania, who had laid out the lots for downtown Knoxville, naming them after the streets of his native Philadelphia. The McClungs' four children were Matthew, Hugh, Polly and Elisabeth (Betsy). The family home was Statesview, out at rural Ebenezer in west Knox County, designed by architect Thomas Hope. However, Hugh's son Hugh Lawson McClung Jr. lived in the Park City area.

Hugh Lawson McClung Jr., born in 1858, son of Hugh Lawson McClung Sr. and grandson of Margaret White and Charles McClung, was a lawyer, merchant and judge who married Ella Gibbons in 1892, in Knox County. Ella and Hugh had one child, Ellen, born in 1893.

In the 1890s and early 1900s, the family was living at 2118 Bell Avenue, known as Jackson Avenue during their residence and now McCalla. Their house was at the corner of Green Street, today's Kyle Street, in the Poplar Springs subdivision of Shieldstown, which later was incorporated as Park City. Though the house is no longer standing, two craftsman houses from the period still stand nearby, at 120 Keller Street, a block to the west, and at 1940 McCalla Avenue, two blocks to the west, and are illustrated in the chapter on Park City's subdivisions.

The McClungs' McCalla Avenue house was gone by 1917; the Sanborn fire insurance map for that year shows a vacant corner lot. By then they had spent some years traveling and had built a new home, Belcaro, on Black Oak Ridge. Ellen McClung married Thomas H. Berry in the 1920s and had one son.

Joseph Bell of Bell Farms

Joseph Bell, husband of Mary Downing Bell, bought 500 acres of land in 1808 from Moses White, son of James White who founded Knoxville. Bell then bought 1,200 more acres in the area between 1810 and 1824.

The Bell farm has long been remembered in local place names in the vicinity: two Bell Avenues, today's McCalla and Wilson Avenues; two Bell Streets, today's Ben Hur and Bell Streets; Bell Avenue Baptist Church, once located on the corner of McCalla and Bertrand; and two Bell Cemeteries, one still located in a little stand of trees in a residential area, the location of the other uncertain, where deceased Bell family members were buried.

The site of Bell's farm and home can be established without reviewing all the land sales records: likely the farm was bounded or bisected by McCalla Avenue on the north, Wilson Avenue on the south, Ben Hur Street on the east and Bell Street and First Creek on the west. And the Bell family estate house and perhaps other family houses were likely near the little stand of trees not far from loved ones buried in the Bell family cemetery.

It is possible that the Bell family later owned land bounded by Woodbine Avenue on the north, Howard Street (Linden Avenue) on the south, Olive Street on the east and Bertrand Street on the west. Joseph Bell's daughter Sarah and son-in-law Preston Blang at some point inherited or purchased this section of land.

The children of Mary and Joseph Bell, likely born between 1815 and 1830, and raised on the rural lands that became southern Park City, were Margery, Isabella, Margaret, Sarah Anne, Mary, Jane, Joanna and Phillip Bell. Margaret Bell married a Henry, Mary Bell married a Harvey, and Sarah Anne Bell, called Sally, born in 1820, married Shieldstown developer Preston Blang in 1836 when she was fifteen and he was twenty-three. Another Margaret Bell, born around 1800, likely a sister of Joseph Bell, married George Blang in 1818.

Preston Blang of Poplar Springs

Joseph Bell's daughter Sarah and son-in-law Preston Blang farmed and developed a tract of land, inherited or purchased from the Bell family, bounded by Woodbine Avenue on the north, Howard Street (Linden Avenue) on the south, Olive Street on the east and Bertrand Street on the west. Apparently they lived and farmed the land for many years, from the 1850s through the 1880s.

The children of Sarah Anne Bell and Preston Blang included Joseph, Margery and Charles, born between 1838 and 1848. The 1850 Knox County census record lists Preston Blang, thirty-eight, employed as a brick mason, his wife Sarah, age thirty, and their children Joseph A.C., twelve, Margery C.I., seven, and Charles P., two. Also listed in the household were three male laborers around the age of twenty.

Preston Blang, in partnership with John Shields, developed his land into a subdivision called Poplar Springs, consisting of several city blocks, each divided into perhaps ten 50- by 150-foot lots. The boundaries of Shields and Blang's Poplar Springs development were Bertrand Street on the west, Olive Street on the east, East Fifth Avenue on the north and Howard Street (Linden Avenue) on the south. The area became known as Shieldstown.

The 1860s Shieldstown Cemetery is still located on Linden Avenue east of Bertrand Street in Poplar Springs; the 1870s Third Baptist Church once stood on the same block. The 1880s Shieldstown School once stood on the corner of Linden and Olive; the 1890s Park City Presbyterian Church still stands across the street. The 1920s Little Brick Church still stands on East Fifth Avenue just past Bertrand; there were once Shieldstown houses all around it, including on Spring Street, now a service alley to the rear of the church.

A few older houses are still standing in Poplar Springs; none remain from the 1860s or 1870s, but possibly one or two are from the 1880s and 1890s and a few more from the 1900s and 1910s. These are small cottages with arches and pillars, farmhouses with decorative trim, and craftsman foursquares and bungalows.

By 1858, the northern part of the original Blang land, fronting Craig Street, was owned by the Burnett family, who sold a section along Craig Street for the widening of the street, which was then renamed Magnolia Avenue for a lady in the one of the Victorian houses along it, Magnolia Brannum.

JOHN SHIELDS OF SHIELDSTOWN

In 1854, Joseph Bell's heirs sold land to developer John Shields, who was in partnership with Preston Blang, and Shieldstown received its name. The 1859 Knoxville City Directory names residents of a six-block district extending from First Creek east to Bertrand Street. Its primary street was Linden Avenue, then called Howard Street, the main route west to Knoxville or east to Asheville.

The original settlement included the Park City subdivisions Elmwood Park and Poplar Springs, whose 50- by 150-foot lots first appeared on an 1859 survey map. I bought my Elmwood Park lot 130 years later in 1989 and began researching the origins of my house, my Elmwood Park subdivision and the antebellum village Shieldstown.

More had been researched and written about a later subdivision, Edgewood, developed from the late 1880s to the early 1900s, but it was years before I knew of Hazen Hill, East End, Chestnut Ridge, Cold Springs and Lake Park Springs. And the details of Poplar Springs and my own Elmwood Park remained elusive until recently.

Chapter 3

SHIELDSTOWN

SEARCHING FOR SHIELDSTOWN

I first heard of Shieldstown when my family moved into a historic house in the rolling hills of its northern outskirts. The town started out as farmland alongside a creek. By the 1850s, the little town covered six square blocks along the main route from Knoxville to the east. In the 1860s, the muddy terrain of a treeless wartime landscape lay in sight of forts on the bluffs above. At the end of the 1870s, there were 165 houses on a network of neighborhood streets, with Shieldstown home to 721 residents. The 1880s and 1890s brought schools, churches, parks and residential additions. Shieldstown became part of Park City in the early 1900s, which was itself swallowed by Knoxville before the 1920s.

Our house, I would learn, was built within the boundaries of Shieldstown, a few blocks north of the bustling epicenter of churches and cemeteries, shops and schools. The family who built our house had its roots in Shieldstown: they had lived in Shieldstown for decades; their sons had married Shieldstown girls; these families in turn lived next-door to their elders and raised their children where they had been raised; and some of them were buried in the Shieldstown Cemetery. The family's younger daughter married a farm boy from Strawberry Plains and went to live with his family in Knoxville. But they came back to Shieldstown and built a house—our house.

They bought the property in 1909, "unembellished with dwelling," and are listed on the deed, in directories and by their descendants as William Green Black, a conductor on the Southern Railway, and his wife, Isadora Elisabeth Day, who stayed home and kept house. Their five children were Anna Elisabeth, Pansy Annalee, Claude Simon, Frances (known as Red) and Helen Margaret. In white dresses and white sailor suit, they regard us quietly from childhood portraits that hang in their parlor—our parlor. Annie married an Oakwood boy, raised six children and built the bungalow next-door; her husband, Harry, kept a store. Pansy married, moved away and died in childbirth. Claude had a bungalow out near Chilhowee Park and worked for the railroad like his father. Red married and traveled all over the country. Helen stayed single and worked in a hospital all her life.

They were long gone when we bought their eighty-year-old house, christening it Blackberry Corner for them and for the blackberries twining the fence. For the first fifteen years we were there, I occupied myself with learning about the people who had lived in our in house. We met the descendants of the house's original owners, invited them on a teatime tour, listened to stories about life in the early days and learned whose rooms had been whose. I tucked their family histories into oak file cabinets in their old library and hung their portraits, solemn in waistcoats and pompadours, in their old parlor.

We learned all we could about the land around Blackberry Corner: what it had been like before the bread factory was built, before the trolley went out to Chilhowee Park and before there were houses on dirt roads with half-acre gardens and horses and cows in the meadows. In the earliest histories of our neighborhood, the main roads were Howard Street, Bertrand Street and Bell Avenue. Howard Street was the main road east from downtown Knoxville out into the countryside; Bertrand and Bell were the north-south connectors, running from Mabry to Howard. In an old city directory, a description of Bertrand caught my attention: "from the Catholic Cemetery north to Shieldstown." I had never heard of Shieldstown—nor had anyone else I asked.

FINDING SHIELDSTOWN

I wondered about, searched for and inquired after the mysterious Shieldstown, at the northern end of Bertrand Street, wherever that was in the nineteenth century, the road from the Catholic Cemetery. Today, Bertrand Street begins on Bethel Avenue next to a row of old cemeteries, slopes and jogs through several blocks of Park City houses and rises to Dodson Street at the foothills of a little ridge. Was Shieldstown up on the ridge where Bertrand ends today? In the middle of Parkridge Park where Bertrand jogs to the east? Was Shieldstown named for John Shields? Was his residence part of the town? He could have been a civic leader who actually lived in Shieldstown, or he might have been an urban planner who provided land but made his home elsewhere. Years passed, and the questions remained unanswered.

One day I happened on an 1880 online census for Shieldstown, 165 households east of First Creek. There I found a listing for John H. Day, farmer, and his wife, Anna, keeping house, with a large brood of children, including daughter Isadora, nine. Residing in the elusive Shieldstown of yesteryear were the ancestors of our house! Dora Day, who married Green Black and built our house, had spent her childhood in Shieldstown. Where was her house? What was it like? I began searching in earnest for the edges of Shieldstown, perusing books and maps, studying streets that have changed their names and their directions, and when I found Shieldstown, I walked its streets, peering among the factories and cemeteries for a house that could have been Dora's, one that dated back to the 1880s, perhaps a farmhouse with gingerbread trim. I saw broad bungalows with stained-glass sidelights, farmhouses with plain or carved trim and small cottages with arches and columns. Could one have belonged to the Days?

I began to compile the information I had from books on my shelves, papers in my files and maps at the library. I learned that the land east of White's Creek was once the farm of Moses White, early settler and son of James White, founder of Knoxville. Joseph Bell then bought land in the area, still remembered in local place names: Bell Cemetery in the middle of someone's backyard and four streets called Bell that once made a circuit around his farm. When the heirs subdivided the farm in the 1850s, John Howard Shields bought part of the land, eventually developed as Shieldstown. At some point, White's Creek was renamed First Creek, though part of the Shields land was called White's Pasture for years to come.

Shieldstown was, evidently, in the 1850s, a six-block residential district extending from First Creek east to the crossroads of Bertrand and Howard, including, at some point, the Shields home. Today there is nothing left of the 1850s Shieldstown settlement between First Creek and Bertrand Street, except sidewalks and parking lots, and where Shieldstown houses might once have stood near the creek are the warehouses of a plumbing supply company. But on a little knoll not far from First Creek, to the southeast of Bell and Howard, is a stand of tall trees, catawbas and maples, remnants of someone's garden. And at the back of the abandoned garden is one old gnarled grandfather tree that defies identification, ancient and stout, thick branches spreading, a species we have never seen. A Shieldstown house stood there.

By the 1860s, Shieldstown was in the middle of a civil war. Tennessee seceded from the Union, and the state fairgrounds, located near what is now Chestnut Street on the eastern outskirts of Shieldstown, became the mustering grounds for all east Tennessee Confederate regiments. Shieldstown and the county around it were predominantly Union, but the Confederate Conscription Act of 1862 forced young men of the county into the Confederate army. Two forts were built on the bluffs to the southwest, Fort Huntington-Smith and Fort Hill, occupied by the Union army during the autumn of 1863. From the forts, then as now, one might have a bird's eye view of Shieldstown. At one point, trees and shrubs in the area were burned so that no enemy would be obscured by their foliage, leaving the landscape a muddy plain below the forts. The area that would become East Fifth Avenue, our street, at one point served as a Confederate boundary to the north. There, 125 years after the war, we came upon an unfired handmade bullet that might have fallen from a soldier's pocket. We found it when we were digging in old boundary earth to plant a tree, not realizing then that no tree in sight could be older than 125 years.

After the war, throughout the 1870s, Shieldstown expanded with the construction of schools, churches, parks and homes. The original Shieldstown settlement became part of the Elmwood Park subdivision, established by John Howard Shields on Howard Street west of Bertrand, eventually including more streets. Shields and neighboring landowner Preston Blang also established the Poplar Springs addition along Howard and Islington, extending the town another six blocks east of Bertrand to Olive. The crossroads of Bertrand and Howard seemed to form the town center: the Shieldstown Country School stood on Howard, six lots east of Bertrand, flanked by two shops on the corners of Bertrand and Cruze. The community was devout, with several churches: Sanctified Methodist at Bertrand and Islington; Bell Avenue Baptist at Bertrand and Bell; Second Presbyterian on Bertrand north of Bell; and Third Baptist on Howard east of Bertrand. When I walked in the area, I saw a few older houses still standing in the old Poplar Springs district on old Howard Street, today's Linden Avenue, between Bertrand and Olive: small cottages with old-fashioned arches and posts, farmhouses with bits of decorative trim and bungalows from a later era. Some are gone now.

I found the Shieldstown Cemetery on Linden Avenue in Poplar Springs, one of the oldest sections of Shieldstown, when researching families who once lived nearby. The earliest known grave is from 1861, the initials of the deceased scratched on a flat stone with the date. According to the cemetery deeds, R.S.J. Hill and her husband, William Hill, were the owners of Shieldstown Cemetery through the 1870s. William Hill was likely the Reverend Mr. Hill, pastor of Third Baptist Church, three lots to the west of the cemetery, also known as Hill's Chapel. The Hills sold the cemetery to Eliza Gay in July 1879, and in May 1882, Eliza Gay sold the cemetery to William Davis and other trustees, not named. They, or their descendants, may still own it, though they may not know it and appear not to have been maintaining it.

Shieldstown families used the Shieldstown Cemetery from the 1860s through the 1940s. Not all the graves were marked with engraved stone markers; some were marked with plain stone markers, with rocks or plantings or not at all; after all, families knew where their loved ones were buried. Moses Lusby, killed in the Mabry-Lusby feud mentioned by Mark Twain in *Life Along the Mississippi*, lived in Shieldstown and was buried in the Shieldstown Cemetery in 1882.

By the 1880s, Shieldstown had grown to 721 residents living in 165 households, with a mingling of races and classes. The 1880 census listed 104 white families and 61 black or mulatto families living next-door to each other. About one-fourth of the Shieldstown households were headed by black or white women, another fourth by black men and one-half by white men. Men were identified by a trade or profession; women, even widows and single women living alone, were listed as "keeping house." It may be that they were able to make a living for themselves with the chickens and gardens outside their doors. The few women who worked at other tasks or outside the home were employed in the capacity of cooks, housekeepers, seamstresses or washerwomen. Only a few children were listed as being "in school." Typically, boys were working alongside their fathers or apprenticed to a trade by age thirteen.

Most of the Shieldstown men and boys worked with their hands. They were employed as barbers, blacksmiths, boatmen, bricklayers, butchers, carpenters, cabinet makers, carriage makers, chair caners, conductors, draymen, drivers, farmers, fishermen, gardeners, harness makers, hucksters, ironworkers, laborers, mail carriers, painters, peddlers, plasterers, printers, saddlers, shoemakers, stonemasons, teamsters, traders, wagoners and well diggers. They also worked for brickyards, drugstores, factories, foundries, gasworks, livery stables, lumberyards, markets, mills, quarries, railroads, slaughterhouses, tan yards and tobacco manufacturers. But some Shieldstown residents owned the businesses where they worked, and the town also had an herb doctor, office worker, teacher, manufacturer, two ministers, five merchants and several clerks. The latter lived side by side with those of the working class, merchants and ministers next-door to day laborers.

By the 1890s, fashionable residential districts were planned: the East End Addition to the east, Elmwood Park extending north and Edgewood farther north. Among the East End homes were "fourteen elegant residences" at the southeast corner of the state fairgrounds (and wartime mustering grounds) near Chestnut Street, with more 50- by 150-foot lots for further development on the grounds. At the same time, elegant houses were being built along Magnolia Avenue as well. Today several large houses still survive in the East End area, and the historic houses of Elmwood and Edgewood, some of them George Barber designs, are on the National Register of Historic Places, mine included.

The main east–west route through town was still called Howard Street where it lay between First Creek and Olive but was dubbed Linden Avenue east of Olive. With the eastward expansion, the intersection of Olive, Linden and Howard became a community hub, replacing the old crossroads of Howard and Bertrand. The Armstrong School occupied the block bounded by Linden, Olive and Parkview, and at the same corner in 1891 was built a brown brick church that is still standing—Third Presbyterian, later known as Park City Presbyterian. Throughout the latter decades of the nineteenth century, mule-drawn streetcars were replaced by electric; the Mabry-Bell line ran out to the East End property and back via Mabry Street and Bell Avenue (later Vine and McCalla); and the Elmwood Trolley ran out to Chilhowee Park and back on East Fifth Avenue and Washington Avenue.

I read the census records and city directories for nineteenth-century news of the ancestors of my house. In the 1880 census, where I found them, Anna Elisabeth Davenport was close to fifty years old and her husband, John Henry Day, was around seventy. They had been married for over thirty years and were the parents of a large family of children with a wide range of ages, from toddlers to twenties: Charlotte, Sarah, Henry, John, Alexander, Charles, Cordelia, Lafayette, Isadora, William and Martha. The Day children grew up in Shieldstown and intermarried with neighboring families: Henry and William married Burnett girls; Sarah and John married into the Moore family, John more than once; Cordelia and Martha married two Roth brothers; and Charles, the son of a Davenport, married back into the Davenports. Isadora married into a Knoxville family and moved away from Shieldstown but came back.

Anna Davenport Day died in 1883, leaving five children at home: Cordelia, seventeen; Lafayette, fourteen; Isadora, twelve; William, nine; and Martha, five. Cordelia married later that year, Lafayette a few years later and the others during the 1890s. By 1903, John Day was making his home with his daughter Isadora, Mrs. William Green Black, and her family at 102 Pearl Place, Oakwood, where he lived until the close of 1908. Perhaps it is significant that only a few months later, near the end of the summer of 1909, Dora and Green Black bought property near where her family had lived. By the autumn of 1909, they were building the high white house at 1702 East Fifth Avenue, two blocks from where

John H. Day had spent his twilight years with his younger children before their marriages. The back of the East Fifth Avenue house overlooked Spring Street, where Dora may have lived as a young girl, where her father's last home had been, in the midst of extended family homes.

By 1909, when our house was built, a new era had come to the neighborhood: Victorian gingerbread designs were giving way to Colonial Revival styles, and the dirt roads of Shieldstown were being paved into the Elmwood Park Addition. Park City had incorporated all. Decades had passed, and the city had changed, but when we arrived eighty years later, the high white house still stood on its hill and the name Elmwood Park was still on its deed, relics from the ancient past. Our house was around the corner from downtown Park City, with a school, a church and a bread factory that had been there for most of the century. Park City was a quaint term that had all but disappeared from the local vocabulary, and Shieldstown was not even a glimmer in anyone's mind. But Shieldstown still existed on the yellowed pages of the library tomes where I went to research my home and the surrounding hills. And that was where I found that Shieldstown had been right in my own backyard.

The Octagon House

The location of the Shields residence continued to intrigue me—a house significant enough to be mentioned in city directories as a landmark, that of John Howard Shields, was located near First Creek, "one north of Howard" in the 1850s. One what? One mile, one block, one street, one house? And which street was Howard? There is no Howard Street today. From old maps I learned that Howard Street was the old name for the section of Linden Avenue that runs through the Elmwood Park and Poplar Springs subdivisions, between First Creek and Olive Street.

It became clear that the Shields house must have been somewhere north of Linden, somewhere near First Creek. First Creek winds its way past our neighborhood, curves at the ballpark and flows through bottomland to the river. An 1886 pictorial map shows a lone house at the curve—the Shields house? I gazed into the rocks and rushes of First Creek as we crossed a bridge to a ballgame at Caswell Park. Was it here?

Over the years, I researched Shields history, hoping to learn about the family, their house and life in the town named for them. I found that John Howard Shields was born in 1829 in Sevier County, Tennessee, the son of first cousins Eliza Shields of Maryland and Samuel Shields of Tennessee. His wife was Margaret Amanda McMillan, born in about 1834, daughter of Mary Littleford and Alexander McMillan of Virginia, progenitors of a local McMillan family whose land extended from the Wooddale settlement to the Lake Park Springs subdivision, just east of Shieldstown. Margaret Amanda McMillan and John Howard Shields were married in January 1852 and had ten children born between 1853 and 1873: Ella, Eliza, Samuel, Mary, Alexander, Margaret, Lawrence, Anna, William and Destovin.

A breakthrough came when I learned of longtime *News Sentinel* columnist Lucy Curtis Templeton, a former Shieldstown resident who reminisced about her life in 1880s Shieldstown in a dozen of her "Country Calendar" columns during the 1940s and 1950s. Eagerly I began to read these Xerox copies of clippings from library files. To my delight and amazement, one of the columns described the Shields house and provided its location: an antebellum octagonal house on a little hill that later became the site of Catholic High and Pellissippi College, 1640 Magnolia Avenue in downtown Park City, one block from my house!

Now I could imagine the Shields family there, from the era I first learned of them in the 1859 city directory and read their names in the 1860 census record: the wealthy young father and mother presiding over their Octagon House on its grassy slope, perhaps with a rose garden, in sunshine, with the children—Ella, six, and Eliza, four—in curls, full skirts and ankle-strap shoes, and baby Samuel in a white dress, wheeled in a wicker pram. The other children were yet to be born, and the rest of the Shields' family history was yet for me to find.

I continued my research, assisted greatly by the publication of digital maps of the area on library websites. The Octagon House was built on property purchased in 1854 as part of a 152-acre tract running alongside First Creek, according to the description with an 1859 survey map of the property owned by the McClung Historical Collection. The map shows a rough plan of the Octagon House, with its eight-sided exterior, thick walls and cross-shaped interior, located on the north side of Howard

Street, with two curved drives leading from the house to the street, toward intersections with Bertrand on the east and Myrtle on the west. The house occupied today's 1600 block of Linden Avenue, the backside of Pellissippi College.

Also shown on the 1859 survey map are several other farms across Howard Street, south of the Shields property, but also right along the street front, the rudiments of the new Elmwood Park subdivision: thirty-five 50- by 150-foot plots of land surveyed and marked, along the south side of Howard Street, extending west from Myrtle to Bertrand. The 50- by 150-foot numbered plots continue across Bertrand into Poplar Springs. These subdivisions, including mine, were much older than I had thought.

By 1860, Shields owned a total of 2,500 acres in the district, according to census records. The access roads and the lay of the land are shown on Orlando Poe's Civil War topographical map of the area from 1863 to 1864. The Octagon House was surrounded by fields, some of them

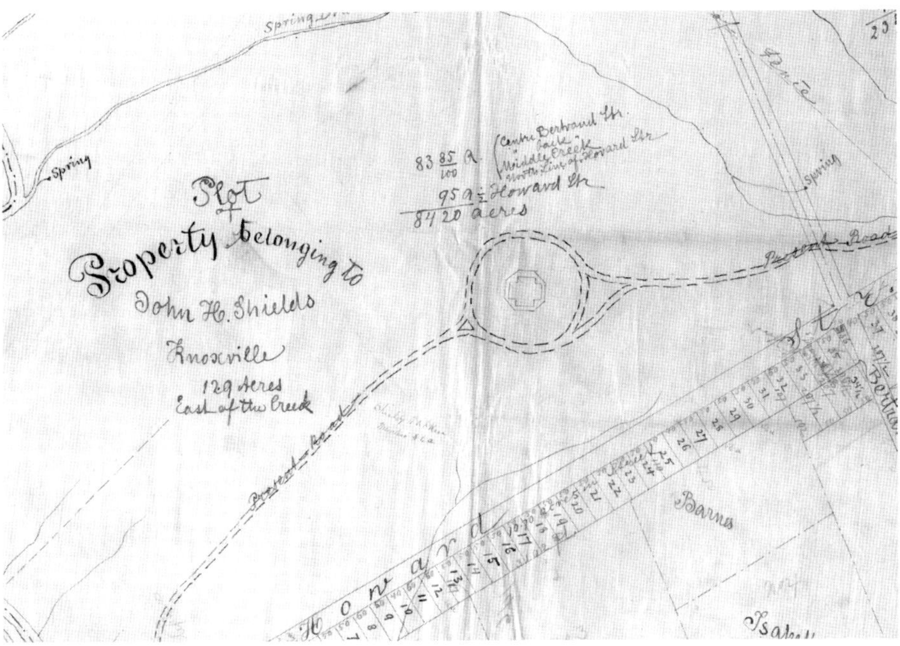

Survey map of John Shields property, 1859. *Photo courtesy of the McClung Historical Collection, Knox County Public Library.*

extending north into White's Pasture, where Caswell Park is now located, and beyond, north to Jefferson, part of an old Shieldstown subdivision where early residents lived a decade or two before the Edgewood Land and Improvement Company began building George Barber design houses there.

Ruth Rodgers, granddaughter of Mr. and Mrs. George M. Branner, who later owned the Shields property, described the property boundaries to Templeton, published in a 1948 column: "I can tell you what Grandmother told me. The little settlement was called Shields' Town because it was next to the Shields' place. The property extended from Bertrand Street west to the creek and from old Howard Street north to Jefferson Avenue."

Readers of a "Country Calendar" column in 1948 learned more about the Octagon House and the family within, as I did when I read it sixty years later in 2008. When the Civil War came to Shieldstown, the Octagon House did not fare well. Rogers recalled what became of it: "On the Shields place before the war, there was a large octagonal house, which was burned by the Federal troops during the 1863 Siege of Knoxville."

On reading this, my thoughts turned to the young landowner and father John Shields, then thirty-four, and his wife, Margaret Amanda, thirty, with small daughters in her arms, Margaret born that year and Mary the year before, no longer at home in the Octagon House. I wondered about their bewildered children Ella, nine; Eliza, seven; and Samuel, four. What was it like to live through the Civil War? And what became of this family?

The Shields house may have stood in its place somewhat past the actual Siege of Knoxville: the Poe map shows the Octagon House and all other structures in the vicinity of Shieldstown marked with Union blue. During the Siege, Federal troops took over the Octagon House, apparently still occupying it in 1864, then likely burned it on their way out of town.

The burned ruins of the Octagon House remained for the next twenty years, visible to families around it, an eyesore to the neighborhood, the blackened foundation eventually overgrown with grass, shrubs and trees. Templeton, who grew up in the next block, remembered seeing and hearing about the charred remains and mentioned this fate of the Octagon House in one of her newspaper columns.

Sometime in the 1880s, the Branner family graded the land and built two Victorians on the property. "It was over a portion of the site of the Shields Octagon House that Grandmother built her residence, now the Catholic High School," Rogers wrote to Templeton, who published her remarks in 1948. "You may recall that the trees that had mounds on them—well, Grandmother said those trees had grown up in the old foundation after the war, and when the place was graded, she had the mounds left around the trees, so as not to lose them."

The pair of Victorian houses built by the Branners on the old Shields property faced not the main thoroughfare, Howard Street, as the Octagon House had, but what had been a short country access dirt road to the north called Craig Street, also known as Magnolia. In later years, a bridge was built over First Creek, connecting Shieldstown's Magnolia Avenue with Knoxville's Park Avenue. For a while, both are said to have been called Park Street, but then both were renamed Magnolia.

The two Victorian houses were built side by side but a block apart, occupying the 1600 and 1700 blocks of Magnolia Avenue. One was for the widowed Mrs. George M. Branner at 1640 Magnolia Avenue, the site of the Octagon House ruins, the elegant Victorian later the site of Catholic High, eventually replaced with a modern structure, and now the site of Pellissippi College. The other Victorian was for son H. Bryan Branner, mayor of Knoxville, at 1724 Magnolia Avenue, now the location of a small strip shopping center. The two 1880s Victorian houses stood prominently on Magnolia Avenue in Park City until the 1950s, when they were torn down and replaced with the present structures.

Chapter 4

EASTPORT

During the 1840s, a small village called Eastport was developing on the outskirts of Shieldstown's farms and roads, in a wooded hillside area to the southeast. Established in the 1840s for free African Americans by devout and wealthy landowners, Eastport soon had a church, school, houses and graveyards on its winding dirt roads, paths and trails. A hint of rural Eastport can still be found today in its pocket of narrow backroads, woodsy and hilly, within a secluded residential section apart from the rest of the sprawling city.

An 1895 Knox County map places part of Eastport in an area of Park City that was later known as Poplar Springs: east of the Confederate Cemetery at 1917 Bethel Avenue near Keller Street; north of the Eastport Cemetery (Oddfellows) at 2001 Bethel Avenue; and also south of Bethel Avenue, extending outside the eventual Park City limits. The Eastport School, built in 1932 at 2036 Bethel Avenue, is also inside this district.

Today, Eastport roads have been paved and widened, some more so than others—Keller, Fuller, Wilder, Harold and Nelson Streets, and Surrey and Bethel Avenues. Eastport place names have survived the two centuries: Eastport School at Bethel and Surrey; Eastport Park at Bethel and old Wilder; and most recently, the Residences at Eastport, on the site of the school and park, making use of the historic school.

Eastport School, 2036 Bethel Avenue, 1932. *Photo by Margery W. Bensey.*

The Underground Railroad

Eastport is said to have been a stop on the Underground Railroad. The town is now—and no doubt was even more so then—a wooded, secluded area near main routes out of the county, such as Rutledge Pike, Dandridge Pike and the convergence of roads at Five Points; the tributaries of creeks along the river; and ferries across rivers throughout the county. For enslaved persons traveling by foot, cart or boat, the location had benefits.

Eastport's connections to safety included a pocket of sympathizers living south of the Tennessee river as well as the vast network of abolitionists in the free states north of the Tennessee border. Eastport's church, built on Fuller Street in 1845, was a station on the Underground Railroad, helping enslaved persons travel to safe locations, usually Kentucky and Ohio.

Fugitives traveled on foot at night through woodlands and swamplands, stopping to rest in tunnels or caves and receiving food and shelter for the night in barns, homes, churches or schools. The distance between one station to the next might be ten to twenty miles, and messengers were sent ahead to alert stations of imminent arrivals.

Fugitives might also travel by wagon, train or boat, with transportation or ticket money donated by individuals or organizations. These benefactors also provided clothing, lodging in cities and help finding jobs.

The Underground Railroad sent hundreds of enslaved persons north to safety each year, possibly as many as 100,000 between 1810 and 1850. The network included African American freedmen, members of the African Methodist Episcopal Church and the Society of Friends and individuals from all backgrounds who assisted with the movement.

Knowledge of this movement often comes through oral history, as has been the case with Eastport's involvement. Those assisting fugitives likely knew only of local efforts but not the greater network and put little in writing, as was necessary for their efforts to be successful.

After the Emancipation Proclamation freed more African Americans, some stayed in Knox County and joined earlier settlers in Eastport.

EASTPORT'S CHURCH, 1845

Eastport's church was the Warner Tabernacle, an African Methodist Episcopal church built in 1845 on Fuller Street south of Bethel on land that was donated to the church. The church is said to have been a center for Eastport's social activities, as churches often were in the nineteenth century, especially in small settlements. It was a center for educational activities as well; records show that until a school could be built, Eastport's children attended classes at the church. When the school was built, it was next to the church.

The Greater Warner Tabernacle, as it came to be called, stood on Fuller Street for 122 years. The church was rebuilt in 1910 following storm damage, then remodeled and improved over the years. The congregation moved from Eastport in 1967 to 3819 Speedway Circle in Burlington, outside Park City, and then in 1987 to the old McCalla Avenue Baptist Church at 3800 McCalla Avenue, its present location, though the street is now known as Dr. Martin Luther King Jr. Boulevard.

Eastport's School, 1860s

The first school for Eastport children met in the cellar of Eastport's church, the AME Zion Warner Tabernacle. The first known Eastport School building was a high school built by 1869 and listed that year in the Knoxville area city directory. An 1895 Knox County map shows Eastport School north of what was then Brabson's Ferry Road. Other records show Eastport School on Fuller Street in 1905. A graduation program survives from 1916, the year four girls graduated from Eastport High School: E.M. Bridges, F.A. Senters, E.M. Stafford and M.E. Wilkerson. Since Eastport by then had been incorporated into Park City, the school was also cross-listed as Park City High School.

Eastport Elementary School, still standing at 2036 Bethel Avenue, was built in 1932 and educated Eastport children for over sixty years. The school closed in 1995, and the building sat vacant for over fifteen years, until restoration began to transform the historic school into a senior citizens' community center with an adjoining apartment complex. The Residences at Eastport opened in 2012, the eightieth anniversary year for Eastport Elementary.

Eastport Families, 1860s–1880s

The 1869 *Knoxville City Directory* lists Eastport residents of African descent, and directories throughout the late nineteenth and twentieth centuries continue to identify Eastport as an African community. Little is known about the community in its early days; area newspapers from 1876 reported meetings of an Eastport Republican Organization and a Hayes and Wheeler Club of Eastport residents.

By 1880, the little village consisted of 149 residents living in thirty-four households, according to the Knox County census for Eastport. Family names of Eastport residents included Bayless, Britain, Bow, Brown, Carter, Chandler, Charlton, Cocke, Delaney, Frazier, Fullinlove, Glenn, Gordon, Henry, Hopewell, Humes, Ivins, Jarnagin, Langdon, Lilison, Lusk, Luty, Martin, McMillan, Mitchell, Montgomery, Nelson, Runnels, Russell, Scott, Scruggs, Sliger, Smith, Thomas, Waisman and Woods.

EASTPORT'S CEMETERY, 1880S

Eastport's cemetery was established from four parcels of land purchased between 1880 and 1885, two of them from Oddfellows chapters, hence the name Oddfellows Cemetery. The seven-acre site is located at 2001 Bethel Avenue. Some well-known citizens buried there include the Reverend Mr. George Washington LeVere, businessmen Clement Jarnigan, John White, Cal Johnson and his two wives, and Melvin Patterson and his daughter Annie Ruth Patterson Booker.

Chapter 5

CIVIL WAR COMES TO PARK CITY

Near where my neighbors and I live in Park City, a war was fought. Most of the neighborhood in the early 1860s consisted of the meadow known as White's Pasture and a village called Shieldstown. But the Civil War came to our neighborhood: soldiers mustered and camped and their families endured where our houses were later built.

We live in what was then the Confederate States of America. Our northeast-facing hillside corner property was on or near a Union boundary. When we go out for the paper, or sit on our steps, or mow our hillside lawn, we stand where the family who built our house stood for their sepia portraits 100 years ago, where a family before them lived in an earlier house 125 years ago and where soldiers walked and camped 150 years ago.

My family property is located in what was then the back field of a wealthy Confederate whose 1854 Octagon House stood about one hundred yards away from where my 1909 Colonial Revival now stands. When the Federals arrived, they took over the Octagon House, then later burned that house to the ground, along with other Confederates' houses. I can imagine Union soldiers marching up the hillside to take over the Octagon House, their uniforms blue with brass buttons, possessing the steps and porches. I can imagine the blaze that consumed the Octagon House when they set it on fire, a block away from mine, decades before mine was built. I have seen fires in my neighborhood, and I can imagine the black smoke poisoning a sky already gray with soot and rain, leaving the charred ruins of the Octagon House an eyesore, and perhaps an example, for the next twenty years. On that site today is a small college campus; I have hurried through its halls to teach writing classes. And I always remember and have told my students that 150 years ago, a secessionist family lived on that slope in the Octagon House.

Not far from our property, just seven blocks east, on a route my family and friends have taken on some of our walks, is an area with historical significance. This parcel of land along Chestnut Street was once known as east Knox County's fairgrounds and then, at the onset of the Civil War, became the mustering place for all Confederate soldiers in east Tennessee. After the war, the area was developed as the East End Addition and populated with elegant Victorians. Years later, during the heyday of Park City, these declining Victorians gave way to modern designs, houses large and small, American Foursquares and Craftsman Bungalows, built throughout the past century. But 150 years ago, during the Civil War, this patch of earth two miles from Knoxville, just past Shieldstown and Eastport, was where all Confederate soldiers in east Tennessee are said to have assembled, trained and prepared for battle.

On another walk to the south, we can see a bluff above our neighborhood to the southwest, with an elementary school, Green Academy, on the site of Civil War–era Fort Huntington-Smith. A historical marker on the school grounds tells the fort's history. Our family ventured up there one day to read it. The view from the fort site is breathtaking: wide blue skies extending forever over the plane of Knoxville and its ridges, rivers and railroads that to this day divide the twenty or so separate towns that were incorporated into the current metropolitan area. When we stood on the precipice of Green Academy and looked out over Shieldstown directly below, we had the same view of the land between the creeks and hills as did those who stood sentry at the fort 150 years ago. We saw paved streets, warehouses, 100-year-old houses and 150-year-old trees, brush and shrubs. They saw dirt roads, farmhouses, small cottages and a bare, burned wartime landscape devoid of trees or shrubs.

Tennessee's Secession 1861

Residents of Knox County's farms and towns were likely dismayed when they learned of South Carolina's secession from the Union five days before Christmas 1860. And with the new year came the news that the Tennessee State Legislature was considering steps toward Tennessee's secession. Mississippi, Florida, Alabama, Georgia and Louisiana all seceded within a two-week period in January and then Texas at the first of February.

At the time, secessionists were a minority in Tennessee. Most residents of Knox County were not passionate about secession; a whole Union was more important than states' rights. The region had no industrial or plantation economy dependent on slave labor. Most of Knox County's twenty thousand white residents and freedmen were small farmers or storekeepers who did not require or choose such labor. However, in the center of predominantly Unionist Knox County, residents of the small-town county seat, Knoxville, were strongly secessionist.

In early May, the Tennessee State Legislature voted to join the Confederacy. Statewide, the vote was 105,379 for secession and 47,233 against. Of those minority votes, 30,000 were from residents of east Tennessee counties, who considered seceding from Tennessee.

In Knox County, among residents of country farms and towns, including Shieldstown, only 439 voted for secession; 2,829 were against it. In the county seat, Knoxville, however, the vote was 777 to 377 in favor of secession.

Companies of volunteers were organized by Governor Isham Harris to serve the Confederate government, and Unionist east Knox County's small hamlet Shieldstown provided the mustering place for all Confederate soldiers in east Tennessee, on the old fair grounds at Chestnut Street, then two miles east of Knoxville.

Shieldstown in Secession 1861

In the heart of Shieldstown, the village named for his family, John H. Shields, his wife, Mary Amanda McMillan, and the first few of their ten children were living at dwelling No. 543, then fronting the 1600 block of

Howard Street, now Linden. Shields had sold lots, established Shieldstown and started the Elmwood Park and Poplar Springs subdivisions to the west and east of his house. A secessionist, he would lose his property to the Federal government before the end of the war. In 1860, he still owned 2,500 acres of land to the north of his house, known as White's Pasture. His land is the location of today's Pellissippi College, Caswell Park, Park Place Condominiums and also my property, Blackberry Corner.

John Burnett, resident of nearby dwelling No. 547, owned forty acres. James M. Davis, a widowed father of three and brother of my northern great-great grandfather, lived in dwelling No. 576. He owned and farmed four thousand acres, worked as a blacksmith and was raising two teenage sons and a daughter alone. Moses Lusby and his wife, Sophia Moore, longtime residents of Mabry Street in Mountain View and later Bertrand Street in Poplar Springs, had a large family, including boys in their teens. They lived in dwelling No. 582 and owned one hundred acres.

Benjamin Burnett lived in dwelling No. 600 and owned fifty acres along today's 1900 block of Magnolia Avenue. A decade or so after the war, he sold part of his family's land for the widening of Shieldstown's old narrow Craig Street into the avenue. Joseph A. Mabry, husband of Laura Churchwell and father of fourteen, was the largest landowner in the area, with sixty-one thousand acres, including Cold Springs Farm and its early 1800s estate house on old McCalla Avenue, or Rutledge Pike, in what became Park City. In 1858, he built another house on Mabry Hill, Dandridge Avenue, in the town of Mountain View, which figured prominently in both the Confederate and Federal defenses due to its vantage point.

These east Knox County families, along with families throughout the nation, were likely sobered to learn of the events of April 1861: the bombardment of the United States Army's Fort Sumter by the Confederate army, the opening engagement of the American Civil War. It was after this event that Tennesseans, rather than strengthening their Unionist views, shifted to a secessionist stance. Virginia seceded within days of the firing on Fort Sumter; Arkansas and North Carolina followed in May and Tennessee in June, the last to secede, effective June 8, 1861.

Federal forces were commanded by United States Army general Ambrose E. Burnside, who was instructed by United States President

Lincoln to enter east Tennessee and secure it for the Union—though it was more than two years before he did so.

Confederate forces were commanded by Confederate army general James Longstreet, who was instructed by Confederate president Jefferson Davis to establish the District of East Tennessee of the Confederate Armies, with General Felix Zollicoffer in charge, and to station guards at every crossroad and railroad with the purpose of moving troops north.

Thus Tennessee was now a Confederate state, and right down the road from Shieldstown, all companies of east Tennessee Confederate volunteers, organized by strong secessionist governor Isham Harris, were mustered at the county fairgrounds. And yet in most of Knox County, and likely in Shieldstown, loyalties remained with the Union.

The Confederate Mustering Grounds

Park City has no historical markers where the Confederate army organized and trained during the early years of the Civil War before the United States Army took over the area. Some historians have searched old records for the location of the old county fairgrounds, later the wartime mustering grounds and then later an enclave of elegant residences. All are gone now.

However, a city ward map from 1924 shows the boundaries of the East End Addition: old McCalla Avenue on the north, Ulster on the south, Cherry on the east and Chestnut on the west. Somewhere within this tract of land were the old mustering grounds where troops prepared for war and the old county fairgrounds where families gathered for leisure.

The location also was given in nineteenth-century newspaper articles noting fairground events, the sale of lots and the route of the Mabry and Bell electric streetcar line on its way to Beaman Lake. The mustering grounds were at or near the corner of old McCalla and Chestnut, east of Five Points.

Today there is no sign of the old fairgrounds where the Confederate army organized and trained before the United States Army took over Five Points. My family has taken neighborhood walks and seen not a trace of the pre–Civil War county fairgrounds, the Confederate mustering grounds or the elegant Victorians of the East End addition that were built on the site during later times of prosperity.

MUSTERING AT SHIELDSTOWN

One wonders who these volunteers might have been, making their way to the Shieldstown mustering grounds: Confederate farm boys and young men from predominantly Unionist east Tennessee counties, walking to enlist past east Knox County farm boys who perhaps continued to work their family land alongside their fathers. Among them might be James M. Davis's sons James and George, in their teens, from my Unionist family, or the Burnett and Woods boys on Bertrand Street near my historic house. The wealthy and prominent Mabry and Shields families were Confederates, but their boys were too young for battle.

Of course, documents exist with the names of the enlisted, including Thomas Humes's 1888 *The Loyal Mountaineers of Tennessee*, and many events of the war are described and clarified by maps, diaries, letters, articles and books written during the century and a half following. The pay for a Confederate soldier ranged from as much as $175 a month for a colonel to as little as $11 a month for a private. The enlisted men received a daily ration and a yearly clothing allowance and otherwise provided for themselves. By the end of the war, it wasn't enough. But beyond a few facts, little is written about what the war was like for residents of the farms and towns of east Knox County, and even less was written about Shieldstown.

Prominent Confederates in the area included C.W. Charlton, William M. Churchwell, John H. Crozier, Colonel David H. Cummings, J.R. Graves, Joseph A. Mabry, William Gibbs McAdoo, Dr. James Gettys McCready Ramsey, John Crozier Ramsey, William H. Sneed, William G. Swan, Campbell Wallace, Benjamin Franklin Welcker and Moses White, of Memphis, who returned for the cause. General Felix K. Zollicoffer, a former Knoxville resident, arrived in June to command all Confederate forces in east Tennessee.

Yet, even though Tennessee was a secessionist state, inhabited by prominent and wealthy Confederates, with Confederate mustering grounds in Shieldstown and Confederate troops guarding its interests, Knox County continued to be inhabited by and influenced by Unionists. Horace Maynard, T.A.F. Nelson and George W. Bridges held seats in Congress. William Gannaway Brownlow, orator, publisher and later governor of Tennessee, was a prominent Unionist, as was Thomas W. Humes, pastor, historian and university president.

At first, the Confederate government was tolerant of Unionists, as their purpose was to win Unionists over to the Confederacy. But before the end of the year, Confederate president Jefferson Davis ordered all the citizens of east Tennessee take an oath of allegiance or leave the country. Some Unionists glibly took the oath, not intending to keep it; others gladly left for Kentucky.

Shieldstown Families: B.F. Welcker

Captain Benjamin Franklin Welcker of Roane County, who had family connections to Shieldstown, mustered into Confederate service in late summer 1861. He was joined by his brother, Senator Henry Inman

Benjamin Franklin Welcker. *Photo courtesy of James Henry Welcker.*

Welcker, who had served in the Tennessee House of Representatives from 1855 to 1856 and in the Senate from 1857 to 1858. These Welckers, whose papers I have inherited, were second cousins of my northern great-grandmother, Mary Anne Inman, whose sons fought on the other side, her youngest, John Henry Davis, in service at age fifteen.

Captain Welcker's older brother, Chancellor James Monroe Welcker, married Margaret Park, daughter of Sophia Moody and the Reverend James Park, whose house has stood downtown at Cumberland and Walnut for two hundred years. Another brother, Chancellor Albert Gallatin Welcker, married Nancy Park White, daughter of Sophia Moody Park and George McNutt White Sr., and granddaughter of Sophia and James Park. The Welckers' sister Catherine Freeling Welcker married General Albert S. Lenoir of Lenoir's Station, later Lenoir City.

Benjamin Welcker married Hester Anne Ish in 1852 but had no living children when the war began. He and his brother Henry were merchants in Kingston, had a farm four miles south on Riley Creek, ran an iron ore operation and sold land and slaves. Ben and Henry recruited like-minded men from Roane County to join them and, in September 1861, formed Company I, Twenty-sixth Regiment, of the Volunteer Infantry, with Ben serving as captain.

These troops were encamped for several months on the old fairgrounds at Shieldstown and on the grounds of the brick Mabry house at Cold Springs Farm. Before doing battle, they reorganized as part of the Fourth Consolidated Tennessee Infantry Regiment and moved to Bowling Green and Russellville, Kentucky. Under the command of General Buckner, they fought in the battle of Fort Donalson, during which they were taken prisoner. Benjamin Welcker was imprisoned on Johnson Island in Lake Erie and Henry Welcker at Camp Chase near Indianapolis. In the summer of 1862, they and most of the officers captured at Fort Donalson were then transported by rail to the Ohio River and then by boat down the Mississippi River to prison at Vicksburg.

After their release from Vicksburg in 1863, they returned to Roane County and formed a cavalry known as Welcker's Silver Grays, with Benjamin Welcker as major. In September, they fought under General Nathan Bedford Forrest at Chicamauga, and in October, Ben's daughter Dixie was born.

Shieldstown Families: J.A. Mabry

In the ridge-top town of Mountain View, prominent citizen Joseph A. Mabry provided grey cashmere uniforms for the first company of infantry and volunteers in Knox County, which ultimately cost $100,000. His Dandridge Pike house, high on Mabry Hill overlooking a wide panorama of countryside, was a Confederate bastion the first two years of the war, with his Cold Springs Farm country home down below providing camp grounds for Confederate soldiers mustering at the nearby fair grounds. But during Federal occupation of the Knoxville area, Mabry amiably switched his allegiance to their cause, and both houses survived. Mabry Hill became an important Federal lookout point, marked on Orlando Poe's 1863–1864 topographical map of the Federal forts and batteries in the area. Because of this alliance, Mabry was not subject to government seizure of property as other Confederates were; his property and both his houses stayed in the family, while other Confederates saw their houses burned and their land sold as enemy property.

Knoxville Families: W.G. Brownlow

At the onset of the Civil War, orator and editor William G. Brownlow spoke out against both abolitionists and secessionists. Once Tennessee seceded, Brownlow shifted his attacks to the Confederate government. In the autumn of 1861, he was forced to cease publishing his opinionated editorials and articles in the *Knoxville Whig* and flee to the mountains. Offered a safe conduct pass to Union lines, Brownlow returned to Knoxville the winter of 1862 only to be arrested and imprisoned. After being escorted to Union lines that spring, Brownlow toured the north, speaking out in public and publishing books and articles on the secession and rebellion. In the autumn of 1863, Brownlow returned to Knoxville following its occupation by Union general Ambrose Burnside and resumed publishing his newspaper under the slightly altered name *Knoxville Whig and Rebel Ventilator*.

BRIDGE BURNINGS 1861

In November 1861, residents of Shieldstown and environs were likely shocked to learn of further wartime violence in the Union burning of railroad bridges to inhibit Confederate rail transport north from Virginia and Georgia. One bridge defied burning, a wooden structure fifteen miles east of Shieldstown over the Holston River at Strawberry Plains in Jefferson County. Its vigilant guard fought off twelve Union men and saved it, a story told in this area for the next 150 years.

This first act of resistance and violence from Union subjects against the Confederate government had drastic results: those suspected of being bridge burners were considered prisoners of war and were imprisoned, exiled and even hanged. Five alleged bridge burners were hanged on site, their bodies left dangling for days in full view of passing trains, and at least one was a case of mistaken identity.

The Knoxville courthouse jail held 150 Unionists, spilling over into an overflow jail nearby. About 1,500 to 2,000 Unionists who may or may not have been involved in the bridge burnings were sent to Tuscaloosa, Mobile and Macon to serve prison terms. William G. Brownlow was one of them, charged with treason, perhaps more for his outspokenness than for being the mastermind behind the bridge burnings.

MARTIAL LAW 1861

The little county seat of Knoxville, population six thousand, was immediately put under martial law, which no doubt had an effect on the surrounding small towns and farms, including the hamlet of Shieldstown.

Residents' houses could be entered at any time by the Confederate army. Citizens could no longer own weapons and were required to turn in their guns and pistols, "even those intended only for sporting use," as Thomas Humes stated in his wartime history, *The Loyal Mountaineers of Tennessee*.

No one could enter or leave the county seat without a passport. Some county residents learned this on their way to church on Sunday morning when they found armed Confederate soldiers guarding the route. A passport was required, signed by a committee of three, upon an oath of allegiance to the Confederacy.

Perez Dickinson, a well-known citizen and merchant for over thirty years, went north on business, with a written permit from Governor Isham Harris, returning on a Saturday evening. On Monday morning, he was arrested and charged, on the word of a Confederate witness, with being born in the north, going to the north and having contact with persons in the north.

Others in the vicinity were tried, fined or jailed for speaking in favor of the Union; treated badly; or even "whipped with hickories," noted Humes. But the Union resistance and violence for which the Confederates had prepared as a result of the bridge burnings did not happen.

Wartime Limitations 1862

As the war continued, citizens left, businesses closed, stores' shelves were depleted, necessities were unavailable and prices escalated. Coffee, usually fifteen cents a pound, cost a dollar; salt, formerly two cents a pound, rose thirty cents; brown sugar, previously two cents a pound, rose seventy cents. Calico fabric was eight times its usual cost, and men's shoes and boots went from ten dollars a pair to twenty.

Gold, silver and bank notes were hoarded and thus passed out of circulation, disappeared and became inflated in value. East Tennessee University closed in 1862 and stayed closed for four years. Children still attended school, but these troubled times interfered with their education.

News came only from Richmond, the Confederate version of events, but energetic Knox County residents often rode over the mountains into Kentucky and came back with facts of the war not otherwise available.

The Confederate Conscription Act 1862

With the 1862 passing of the Confederate Conscription Act following the Battle of Nashville and Governor Isham Harris's flight to Memphis, every man in Tennessee ages eighteen through forty-five was officially a soldier in the Confederate army. One can imagine the dismay at having to join the army of the opposing side or leave one's home.

In Unionist east Tennessee, the law was not always enforced; some Unionists simply declined to appear at the Shieldstown mustering grounds. Others left for Kentucky with the aid of guides who knew the mountain paths between east Tennessee and the United States Army camps in Kentucky. Of these, some were captured and forced into service for the opposing side and perhaps did not live to return home.

Of those who arrived safely in Kentucky, Edward J. Sanford wrote, "They left their homes in companies of ten, fifty, or a hundred, starting at night, sometimes concealing themselves during the day and resuming their journey under cover of the darkness, and at length passed over the border, rejoicing that they were free from the strong hand that would force them to fight against the United States."

SHIELDSTOWN FAMILIES: J.P. DAVIS

The Confederate Conscription Act meant that a boy in my neighborhood, James P. Davis, turning twenty that year, the same age as my college son at this writing, was now officially part of the Confederate army. His widowed father was exempt, as was J.P.'s younger brother George Davis, thirteen. We have never heard what J.P. Davis did during the war, whether he joined the Confederate army or the U.S. Army or kept on working as a blacksmith alongside his father.

J.P.'s father, Shieldstown blacksmith and landowner James M. Davis, was no relation to his neighbors, the Welckers, and may not have known them, though his brother Robert McCorkle Davis married the Welckers' second cousin Mary Anne Inman in Tennessee and migrated to southern Indiana. Their son John Henry Davis, my great-grandfather, joined an Indiana regiment at age fifteen as a drummer boy in 1863, emerging an injured soldier at seventeen in 1865, for which he received a medal and farmland in Indiana for his service. He was J.P.'s first cousin.

J.P. seemed not to live on land of his own; census records show him in the homes of relatives all his adult life. Perhaps he did not serve, or perhaps he served and was impaired.

Knoxville Families: E.J. Sanford

Edward Jackson Sanford of Knoxville, prominent Unionist and businessman, was a young man during the war. He related his story of traveling to Kentucky with a group of Knoxvillians to join the U.S. Army. "For the ostensible purpose of buying beef in the mountain region for the Confederate army," wrote Sanford, "passes were procured by men who employed their time in preparing a boat on the Clinch River, about twenty miles north of Knoxville and secreting it from the watchful eyes of rebel pickets."

The meeting place for the 375 men was Bull Run Creek, fifteen miles north, at midnight on April 18. Confederate army officers learned of the plan and placed guards around the town, which kept seventy-five U.S. citizens from leaving. "I was fortunately one of the few citizens who intended to join the party and were outside of the town before nightfall when the guard was stationed," wrote Sanford. "A carriage ride with my wife early in the evening, as though only for recreation, gave me the opportunity, without suspicion, to pass into the country; and leaving her at the house of a friend five miles from town to return home the next day."

Sanford then walked to the nearby house of a Unionist friend where they were joined by six others. After dark the group walked northward, skirting rebel houses, adding companions from friends' houses. Sanford wrote, "Many were the words of encouragement given and bitter tears shed by mothers, sisters and wives, as those they held dear stepped noiselessly forth from their homes and joined the marching column."

The group numbered seventy-five and met seventy-five more at Bull Run in torrents of rain. Each man had a knapsack with edibles, but only a third were armed, and no one had dry clothes or blankets. With the help of guides, they crossed the Clinch River, Walden's Ridge and the Cumberland Mountains and arrived at the Federal Army Camp at Boston, Kentucky, after six days and nights. Sanford concluded, "In six hours, three companies of as good soldiers as were ever dressed in blue were added to the Sixth East Tennessee Regiment and went forth to do battle for their homes and country."

BLAINE FAMILIES

Humes related the story of a group of young men assembled at Blaine's Crossroads, just over the border in Grainger County, about fifteen miles east of Shieldstown, intending to march north through the mountains but pursued by a Confederate cavalry. Of the six hundred to seven hundred Blaine men, half were taken prisoner and "marched under guard through the streets of Knoxville on their way to jail in the South, for the crime of trying to escape enforced service against the United States."

Humes pondered, "How many of the prisoners, most of whom were only just old enough to be included in the conscript law, ever saw their homes again, it is impossible to say." He further speculated that some died in a Georgia prison, or on the way to it, or while in Confederate service, and that few escaped to return home. And thus it likely also was with Shieldstown boys.

EXILE AND AMNESTY 1862

Humes described further the fate of those who refused conscription: "But a Sabbath past, they brought twenty Union men out of jail, arms tied behind them with strong ropes, and marched them with bayonets to the depot, cursing and insulting them, and sent them off to Tuscaloosa to be held as prisoners of war. To have seen them coming out of the jail yard and entering the street would have brought tears from the eyes."

After enough Union families had been exiled, jailed, banished or left for Kentucky of their own volition, few farmers were left to cultivate the fields and provide food for the Confederate army, so the Unionists were asked to return. If the Unionists didn't accept the amnesty, their wives and children would be uprooted from their homes and sent to them in the north at their own expense. Few chose to return, and some families were sent north from their homes on very short notice.

The Brownlows and Maynards were two such families, given a day's notice to join their heads of household William G. Brownlow and Horace Maynard in Cincinnati, where their political speeches and actions continued to reach the attention and arouse the annoyance of Confederate leaders.

A Union Stronghold 1863

By 1863, residents of Shieldstown and its pastoral hills and dales may have been able to receive up-to-date news of the war, some of it very much first hand, as the U.S. Army at last entered east Tennessee in June. General William P. Sanders arrived with about 1,200 men and encamped his troops in downtown Knoxville at East Fifth Avenue, Henley Street and Gay Street, near the Confederate armory. A skirmish the next day sent bullets whizzing over townspeoples' heads.

In August, the Confederate army left Knoxville to defend the Chattanooga area and fight in the Battle of Chicamauga in late September.

Thus General Burnside arrived in Knoxville in early September with an army of fifteen thousand, totally unopposed. He made his headquarters the John H. Crozier house on Gay Street in downtown Knoxville, later the site of the Farragut Hotel.

Following the Battle of Chicamauga, a significant Union defeat with casualties second only to Gettysburg, Confederate army generals Longstreet and Wheeler made plans to reclaim Knoxville. They marched north on November 16 with a twelve-thousand-member infantry and cavalry.

Burnside had a total of twenty-three thousand troops in east Tennessee, fifteen thousand of them in Knoxville and eight thousand of them elsewhere. On the same day, he moved five thousand U.S. troops from Loudon to Knoxville on a route parallel to the Confederate path, a twenty-four-mile march. The weather was rainy and muddy, and neither side had adequate food, clothing or shoes.

Both sides met at Campbell's Station, the U.S. Army fifteen minutes ahead of the Confederate army. In that battle, the United States had 318 men killed or wounded and the Confederates 174. After that battle, a night march ensued. Federal troops had only quarter rations and their third night without sleep.

A CIRCLE OF FORTS 1863

Captain Orlando M. Poe, chief engineer with the Department of the Ohio, had designed a circle of fortifications and batteries surrounding the Knoxville area, the easternmost of them overlooking the cluster of houses and businesses that formed Shieldstown. Sometimes constructed on the sites of former Confederate forts, these Union forts and batteries were named for officers killed during the Knoxville campaign. To the east, above Shieldstown, were seven ridge-top batteries, encampments or fortifications: Fort Huntington-Smith, Batterie Clifton Lea, Batterie Stearman, Mabry Hill and Fort Hill, all along old Dandridge Pike; and Flint Hill and Batterie Fearns, overlooking the Tennessee River.

Fort Huntington-Smith, on today's Summit Hill Drive, stood atop Temperance Hill in the old town of East Knoxville, incorporated in 1858 between Knoxville and Shieldstown. An elementary school, Green Math and Science Academy, named for Dr. Henry Morgan Green, stands there today. In full view down in the valley below were the Shieldstown settlement and its surrounding farmland and the beginnings of subdivisions that would become Park City. The fort's location can easily be seen from the valley now. Batterie Clifton Lea and Batterie Stearman stood below the fort on the eastern slope of Temperance Hill.

Farther east on old Dandridge Pike beyond Temperance Hill is the ridge-top town of Mountain View, where Mount Calvary Baptist Church and the Mabry-Hazen House Museum offer a spectacular view of the Shieldstown valley and the city to the north and west. The house served as officers' headquarters for both the south and the north during their occupations of the area. Fort Hill, down the slope of Mabry Hill, overlooked today's Rosedale Avenue between Surrey Street and Saxton Avenue. High above the Tennessee River were Flint Hill south of Main Street and Batterie Fearns on the eastern slope of the hill.

Across First Creek from Fort Huntington-Smith stood Batterie Billingsley on today's Commerce Street, between Central and Gay, and a pond north of Vine where the creek was dammed. Batterie Galpin stood farther west, approximately at Henley and Grand, now a large intersection of high-traffic thoroughfares, with Batterie Wiltsie on Vine Street between Walnut and Gay, the site of Immaculate Conception

Catholic Church. Fort Comstock was located just west, where Locust and Vine meet at the very top of Summit Hill, overlooking the railroad yards below. The depots and workshops of the two major railroads, the East Tennessee and Georgia and the East Tennessee and Virginia, were located there. Confederates were thwarted by the Federals firing on the railroad buildings from above and exploding the ammunition stored there.

Farther west across Second Creek stood Batterie Zoeliner on Eleventh Street between Forest and Grand, just north of the Knoxville Museum of Art, Fort Kid and World's Fair Park, with Fort Sanders nearby on Seventeenth Street between Clinch and Laurel, later part of a neighborhood of Victorian houses that, in their decline, became rooming houses for university students. On the university campus were Batterie Noble, at or near the mansion known as Melrose on Melrose Place; Fort Byington on the "The Hill" of the University of Tennessee campus, then East Tennessee University, which closed for the war; and the Union Barracks on the side of the hill between Circle Park and the river.

On the bluffs over the river and in the hills to the south, protecting the river and defending approaches, were Union troops from Michigan, Indiana, Illinois, Ohio, Kentucky and Tennessee. They occupied Cherokee Heights over the river; Fort Higley on Cherokee Trail west of Martin Mill Pike; Fort Dickerson, between Martin Mill Pike and Chapman Highway; and Fort Stanley, east of Chapman Highway. The bluffs over the river are visible from the downtown and university areas, and a wide panorama of cityscape and ridgetops are visible from the forts. Both sides tried to take Cherokee Heights, as much of the countryside was in view and cannon range from there. A Union pontoon bridge at the present site of the Knoxville Riverboat enabled Burnside to control the heights.

The Siege of Knoxville

In November 1863, the west wing of the U.S. Army was stationed behind Thompson-Boling Arena on what is now Neyland Drive, with entrenchments running northwest past Melrose Hall on the University of Tennessee campus and up the hill to Fort Sanders at the corner of Laurel Avenue and Seventeenth Street.

The Third Creek valley west of Twenty-third Street was the domain of the Confederate forces, as were the northern reaches of town beyond the railroad. On arrival in Knoxville, Confederate general Joseph B. Kershaw made his headquarters at Crescent Bend on Kingston Pike, the residence of merchant farmer Drury P. Armstrong.

Longstreet planned an assault on Fort Sanders, where he considered Union defenses the weakest. On Monday, November 23, he invaded Cherokee Heights, expecting artillery fire to reach Fort Sanders 2,400 yards to the north, which it did not, due the quality of gunpowder in those days and the distance required.

That night, Burnside's men burned the Confederate stronghold of North Knoxville. All machine shops and arsenals were set ablaze, as were homes of Confederate sharpshooters, with smoke and flames in the air over North Knoxville visible to residents of surrounding communities, including Shieldstown across the railroad tracks and winding creek. It was an exciting and frightening time for all.

Longstreet continued to plan his assault on Fort Sanders, preparing for battle throughout the week.

THE BATTLE OF FORT SANDERS

Fort Sanders was constructed on a rural hillside a mile west of the county seat of Knoxville, three miles west of Shieldstown. Orlando Poe's 1863–1864 topographical map, with present-day streets superimposed, places the fort at Seventeenth Street and Laurel Avenue, the location of Fort Sanders Manor Apartments, a 1920s structure with a courtyard and fountain where I lived as a university student at the age of twenty.

The legend of Fort Sanders has survived for 150 years; most Knoxville residents are familiar with the story. I knew it when I walked the fort's ramparts on my way to classes, through the courtyard, down the steps and along the steep hillside to campus. Shieldstown residents must have known the story too, perhaps parts of the story that we don't know, parts that have been forgotten in the years since.

The fort had earthen walls twelve or more feet high and ditches eight or more feet deep. Although we sometimes have warm Novembers in

Tennessee, this was a freezing cold one, and the ramparts and ditches were glazed in ice. The northwest side was booby-trapped with shrubs, stumps and telegraph wire at knee height. Inside the fort were 335 Union riflemen, 105 artillerymen and twelve cannons.

Longstreet's assault on the fort took place at dawn on Sunday, November 29, the first day of Advent. The 4,000 Confederate troops crouched low and approached the fort in the near darkness, then found themselves tripping over obstacles, stumbling into ditches, falling on top of one another and scaling the icy walls only to be fired on from above. From within their high bastion, the U.S. Army shot 813 Confederate soldiers in twenty minutes.

The soldiers who fell into the ditches and lived surrendered to Burnside. The 813 dead were left there and covered with earth. All university students living in the Fort Sanders neighborhood know this legend, that somewhere under our feet, perhaps in the backyards of the Victorian houses where some of us had rooms, hundreds of soldiers had been lying for just over one hundred years, some of them our age when they died.

Longstreet remained in the area for a few days and then retreated with his army through Jefferson County. Shieldstown residents might have seen them on their way, marching the roads through Knox County.

The Rest of the War

The Union army occupied the Knoxville area for the remainder of the war. Both armies had stripped the area of its foodstuff and livestock. At least half the citizens had left the area. Those who remained had lives of deprivation, with rampant looting, stealing and hunger.

That year, Union general William T. Sherman, based in Chattanooga, marched to Atlanta and Savannah with 100,000 men against 60,000 under Confederate general Joseph E. Johnston, capturing Savannah in December 1864. In Virginia, the Confederates were overpowered by Federal forces at Richmond and surrendered to General Ulysses S. Grant at Appomattox in April 1865.

During and after the war, many Confederate families went north or west or left the country. Their land was confiscated by the government and sold as enemy property, some were not allowed to vote and many were charged with treason or afraid of being charged with treason. For a time they lived nomadic lives, gaining asylum in Cincinnati or Memphis, pressing on toward Texas or California or stopping in Mexico or Peru. They appealed to the government for pardons and went to court to get their land back. Pardons were granted within a year or two, but the return of land might take a decade or more.

Former governor Isham Harris fled to Mexico and then England, fearing treason charges, as his nemesis William G. Brownlow had been elected governor. But in 1867, Harris returned and requested a pardon, which Brownlow delivered.

The Shields Family

It is not known whether John Howard Shields requested a pardon; a John Shields of Greeneville did so; perhaps he went there after leaving the Octagon House. He and his family went north, then west, then left the country, perhaps facing a treason charge or afraid of such a charge. The Shields land appears to have been confiscated by the government and sold as enemy property or in litigation for many years as the Shields family lived and traveled elsewhere.

Orlando Poe's topographical map of the area for 1863 and 1864 shows the Octagon House and all other structures in the vicinity of Shieldstown marked with Union blue, and it seems likely that during their encampment in the Knoxville area, Federal officers were stationed at the Octagon House. It has been said that they burned it, likely as they left the area, though the reason for the burning at that point remains unclear. It was twenty years before the land was developed, the charred ruin long overgrown with grass, shrubs and trees.

The Shields family remained in Tennessee through 1864, according to their son Alexander's birth record, and left in October 1865, according to a note attached years later to their property survey map. A census record shows that their son Lawrence was born in 1867 in a place not named; they lived in Alabama in 1869 and 1870, where their children Anna and William were born. They next traveled north to Cincinnati, Ohio, where their youngest child, Destovin, was born in 1873, then west to California where they turned up in 1880 census records for Alhambra in Los Angles County: Margaret A. Shields, forty-six, and John H. Shields, fifty, with five of their ten children—Mary, eighteen; Alexander, fifteen; Anna, eleven; William, ten; and Destovin, seven.

Margaret, seventeen, and Lawrence, thirteen, were not listed with their parents in Alhambra and may have died before 1880; nor is Samuel, twenty-one, listed; but he may have returned to Knoxville, as a Samuel Shields is listed there. The older daughters, Ella, twenty-seven, and Eliza, twenty-five, likely were married and living in California or Ohio, their states of residence when they arrived at marriageable ages. Ohio is the most likely, since their mother returned there, perhaps to one of their homes; Margaret McMillan Shields died in Cincinnati at the age of seventy in August 1900. John Howard Shields moved on to Jalapa Enriquez, Veracruz, Mexico, where he died at the age of seventy-two in March 1902.

The Welcker Family

Henry Inman Welcker and Benjamin Franklin Welcker promptly sought and received pardons from the government, though restitution of their confiscated land took years.

Their deceased brother Charles Welcker's estate Welcker's Mill, near the little town of Wheat, was in litigation from his death in 1861 until restitution in 1883. His sons William Lewis Welcker II and James Henry Welcker were in school during the war and in college afterward, educated and supported by their uncles Ben and Henry Welcker, who assisted them in recovering their inherited but confiscated land. Following the sale of their land, Will and Jim were able to repay their uncles.

Another nephew, William Thomas Welcker, son of the Welckers' deceased older brother William Lewis Welcker Sr., was a lieutenant in the U.S. Army before the war, stationed in Oregon in the 1850s. He received a dishonorable discharge when he resigned in 1861 to join the Confederate army, so he left the country for Vancouver Island until he could safely travel to the Confederacy with his family. In about 1863, the family boarded a Spanish ship headed south on the Pacific Coast and through the Isthmus of Panama. The family became ill with typhus, of which two children died as the ship lay off the shore of Peru. As the family was Protestant, the children could not be buried in a Catholic cemetery in Peru. And so the father took the little bodies in a rowboat to the beach, dug a grave in the sand with his hands and buried them there.

Benjamin Welcker and his family left for Memphis, Tennessee, and then Acton, Texas. After a five-year exile and lengthy litigation, his land was recovered. The family returned to Roane County in 1870 with baby Henry; Franklin was born in 1872. The family lived on their farm until Ben's death in 1884. By 1886, Ben's widow, Hester, and the children were living in the new Elmwood Park subdivision near the place were Ben and Henry had mustered twenty-five years before. Dixie was married that year in a home wedding to her first cousin Jim. They stayed in Elmwood Park and raised their family at 1501 Linden Avenue, today's Chilhowee Street. James Henry Welcker was a Park City attorney and judge, and his brother William Lewis Welcker was a Fountain City attorney and judge.

Chapter 6

PARK CITY'S VICTORIAN SUBDIVISIONS

After the Civil War and throughout the 1870s, Shieldstown expanded with the construction of schools, churches, parks and homes. The Elmwood Park and Poplar Springs subdivisions, plotted in the 1850s and under siege of war during the 1860s, expanded during the 1870s, populating White's Pasture from First Creek east to Olive and from Linden Avenue north to Woodbine. By 1880, the town had 165 houses that were home to 721 residents, with a mingling of races and classes. Early records show a Shieldstown Country School, which no longer stands, several stores and churches and the Shieldstown Cemetery, on Linden Avenue, with the earliest grave dated 1861.

Further expansion came during the 1880s and 1890s, as the large and elegant residences of the East End Addition were built on Chestnut Street, site of the old country fair grounds and wartime mustering grounds. Also during these decades the Victorian and Eastlake houses appeared on Washington and Jefferson Avenues in the Edgewood and Hazen Hill additions. The turn of the century brought Cold Springs and Lake Park Springs development in the early 1900s. All these residential developments were incorporated as Park City in 1907.

Elmwood Park

Elmwood Park was likely the earliest subdivision in Park City, dating back to the 1850s, bounded by Caswell Park on the north, Bethel Avenue on the south, Bertrand Street on the east and First Creek on the west and incorporating the original village of Shieldstown. Elmwood Park is still a populated subdivision, full of historic houses built throughout the past century; the name is still on the deed to the 50- by 150-foot plot of land with 1909 house that my husband and I purchased in 1989, where my family still lives.

An 1859 *Shields Survey Map* shows thirty-five standard 50- by 150-foot plots of land along the south side of Howard Street (Linden Avenue), east of Myrtle and west of Bertrand, which made up the earliest vestiges of a planned Elmwood Park, corresponding with today's 1800, 1700 and 1600 blocks of Linden Avenue. The 152-acre Shields property lay on the north side of Howard Street, extending west to First Creek and north as far as present-day Jefferson Avenue. Farms belonging to the Blang, Shady, Mabry, Bell, Van Guilder, Saxton and Champion families lay south of the row of subdivision properties.

Area city directories from the 1890s and 1900s show smatterings of new houses cropping up on the dirt roads between woods and fields, and the Sanborn fire insurance maps show the shapes of the houses, with their turrets and bays, verandas and porches, stables and chicken coops.

Two short east–west roads, Craig Street and Pavel Street, were widened, extended and renamed Magnolia Avenue and East Fifth Avenue. These streets were far from being the main thoroughfares they are today, however; Howard Street, Rutledge Pike and Ruggles Ferry Pike to the south served that purpose. In the 1880s, the Elmwood trolley line ran out East Fifth Avenue from the Elmwood Park subdivision to the Chilhowee Park amusement park, and the entire area, residential section and amusement park, became known as Elmwood Park for a while during the 1890s.

Longtime *Knoxville News Sentinel* reporter Lucy Curtis Templeton recalled living in Elmwood Park in the 1880s when it was a fashionable Victorian neighborhood and wrote about her memories in her *Country Calendar* newspaper column. She described the architectural style of the neighborhood's two-story houses.

Queen Anne cottage, 1405 Magnolia Avenue, Elmwood Park. *Photo by Margery W. Bensey.*

Creamer house, 1709 East Fifth Avenue, Elmwood Park. *Photo by Kiernan W. Bensey.*

Blackberry Corner, 1702 East Fifth Avenue, Elmwood Park. *Photo by Margery W. Bensey.*

> *They were chiefly distinguished by a number of porches adorned with spindles and scrollwork, and the upper sashes of most of these windows were outlined in small square panes of colored glass. Inside, the houses displayed a great quantity of golden oak, as well as many fireplaces surrounded by colored tiles and ornate over-mantles containing one or more mirrors.*

The properties were fenced, and along the back fences were sheds for coal and wood on whose flat roofs neighborhood children jumped and played. On the alleys were stables for the families' horses and carriages. The stable on the back alley of our Elmwood house is gone except for the concrete foundation, still there, forming the edge of our driveway with garden beds on either side. The Curtis' stable had a cupola on the roof, still there in 1948 when Templeton wrote, "It was a favorite haunt of mine; one reached it by a ladder, and I used to sit perched up there with a book and orange, and survey the landscape through the cracks of a little louvre with a great feeling of looking abroad into foreign lands." Templeton wrote further of the Elmwood Park landscape:

> *There were a number of vacant lots between the houses, the space adjacent to the creek bank being entirely open; and it was here that the children of the neighborhood assembled at all seasons of the year to spin tops, play marbles and ball, fly kites, ride bicycles and one or two ponies owned by the fortunate. Even at that early age a devotee of the English school of fiction I had christened this place "The Common," and the name stuck. Our elders had a tennis court and we had some small racquets but for some reason never played. It was more exciting out on the Common.*

She described First Creek flowing through the meadow west of Elmwood. "It was a pleasant, countrified stream, and in August many wild flowers grew there, among them the lavender blue ageratum."

Mary Burwell, later Mrs. Clay Brown Atkin, wrote in 1948, "Having read about your column of last Sunday [April 18, 1948], I felt I had to write about Elmwood, for that was its name. I lived there. My father rented a house on East Fifth Avenue—it still stands—and we lived there until our house was finished at 2320 Jefferson Avenue. That house still stands and is still good looking." As a child, Mary considered the house at 2320 Jefferson, built in about 1891, part of the elite Elmwood neighborhood—though that house was actually east of Elmwood, east of Poplar Springs, in the Hazen Hill development.

Atkin further recalled that Shieldstown included Magnolia Avenue, the street was named for Magnolia Branner and for a short time the name of Magnolia Avenue in Shieldstown was changed to Park Avenue, perhaps to match Park Street in Knoxville, across the bridge over First Creek. Later both were changed back to Magnolia. Atkin also observed that Bell Avenue was changed to Jackson Avenue, then McCalla Avenue.

Many of the old related families of Shieldstown lived around the vicinity of Bell Street and Howard Street. Elmwood Park residents included Allen, Aston, Askins, Black, Branner, Brannum, Burnett, Compton, Creamer, Curtis, Davis, Froneberger, Lusby, Mabry, Magby, Ross, Queener, Tauscher, Turk, Shields, Stephens, Welcker, White and Woods families. One of the most notable residents of Elmwood Park was Mrs. Clara Magby, a woman of African descent who lived

Park Place Condominiums, 523 Bertrand Street, Elmwood Park. *Photo by Kiernan W. Bensey.*

Swan Brothers Bakery, 1801 Magnolia Avenue, Elmwood Park. *Photo by Margery W. Bensey.*

during the years 1780–1880 and was listed as one hundred years old in the 1880 Shieldstown census. Her home was on Bell Street near First Creek in Elmwood Park.

Poplar Springs

Some Shieldstown residents were likely living on farms and lands in the Poplar Springs area eastward across Bertrand Street from Elmwood Park before the Poplar Springs subdivision's 1850s development. Moses White, son of Knoxville's founder, owned Poplar Springs land that he donated to East Tennessee College in 1807, though the college was never built there.

The Poplar Springs subdivision was developed east of the original 1850s six-block Shieldstown residential district that became the core of Elmwood Park. Poplar Springs extended that district east from Bertrand

Queen Anne cottages, 1902, 1904 and 1908 East Fifth Avenue, Poplar Springs. The cottage at 1902 was inhabited by a Brooks family in the 1880s but did not survive the 1980s; the one at 1904 burned in the 1990s; and the one at 1908 is still standing and pictured here. *Photo by Kiernan W. Bensey.*

Street to Olive and north to Craig, Spring, Pavel and Briscoe Streets, simple dirt roads back then, but today's paved Magnolia Avenue, Spring Alley, East Fifth Avenue and Briscoe Alley.

Poplar Springs was developed by Shieldstown landowners John Howard Shields and Preston Blang, whose wives, Mary Amanda McMillan and Sarah Anne Bell, were from area families who had farmed the land for decades. An 1859 *Shields Survey Map* shows a row of standard 50- by 150-foot plots of land extending east of Bertrand along the south side of Howard Street (Linden Avenue), which made up the earliest vestiges of the planned Poplar Springs subdivision, the 1900, 2000 and 2100 blocks of Linden Avenue.

New housing plots were being subdivided and developed throughout the 1860s and 1870s, and Burnett family land was sold for the widening and lengthening of one-block-long Craig Street into Magnolia Avenue in the early 1880s. Howard Street to the south, long a main thoroughfare from Knoxville, was renamed Linden Avenue. Some of my older neighbors recalled that these were dirt roads into the 1920s.

Victorian farmhouse, 2004 East Fifth Avenue, Poplar Springs. Note the vine-covered board-and-batten garage. *Photo by Kiernan W. Bensey.*

Businesses began springing up at the little country crossroads of Bertrand and Howard, the original Shieldstown business district. Pickell's Store was located there, listed in the Knox County census record for Shieldstown in 1880, but later moved east to the Five Points business district where Bell Avenue met Olive Street.

Early Shieldstown schools were in or near Poplar Springs: Eastport School built on Fuller Street in the 1860s; Shieldstown School on the southwest corner of Howard and Olive, listed in a city directory in the 1870s or 1880s; and Belleview School on the corner of Howard and Bertrand in the 1890s and at 2143 Linden in 1900. The nineteenth-century Armstrong School, occupying the 2300 block of Linden and Parkview Avenues, between Olive and Spruce, became the Park City High School in 1908 and Park-Lowry Elementary in 1917. All are gone now, though a newer 1932 Eastport School still stands at 2036 Bethel Avenue.

The 1860s Shieldstown Cemetery is still located on old Howard Street, east of Bertrand in Poplar Springs, where early residents of Shieldstown were buried. The gravestone of Moses H. Lusby is there, though the grave of his wife, Sarah Moore Lusby, is at the Confederate Cemetery, near the Mabry-Hazen House on land donated by the Mabrys back when the Lusbys and Mabrys lived near each other and were friends before the tragic shootings. Small family cemeteries belonging to the Bells, Stephens, Woods and other area families are located in backyards throughout Elmwood Park and Poplar Springs, some of them documented by cemetery researcher Robert McGinnis, though few of them are still visible.

The 1870s Third Baptist Church, once affiliated with Shieldstown Cemetery, stood on old Howard Street east of Bertrand, but it is gone now. The Bell Avenue Presbyterian Church stood at Bell Avenue and Bertrand, then in 1891 moved to a new building on the southeast corner of Howard and Olive, retaining its name. Later known as Park City Presbyterian, the church still stands on that corner. The 1928 Little Brick Church still stands at 1912 East Fifth; there were once Shieldstown houses all around it, including on Spring Street, the alley to the rear.

Longtime *Knoxville News Sentinel* columnist Lucy Curtis Templeton recalled Poplar Springs as a rough area called Shieldstown, rather than Poplar Springs, when she was living in the more elite Elmwood Park west of Bertrand in the 1880s. Templeton wrote of Poplar Springs, "This was

Little Brick Church, 1912 East Fifth Avenue, Poplar Springs, 1928. *Photo by Margery W. Bensey.*

an aggregation of very small and old houses, with one or two larger and more modern ones here and there." Reading this, I find myself wishing that houses considered modern in the 1880s, and especially houses already very old then, might have survived.

Poplar Springs children rarely played with Elmwood Park children, Templeton reported. Some of the Poplar Springs children occasionally came over from the other side of Bertrand Street to play on "The Common" by First Creek, especially in the spring during the kite-flying, marble-playing season, though usually just the boys.

Templeton wrote, "The girls never came; they did not seem to play with their brothers as we did." The boys who came played a little more roughly than the Elmwood children, noted Templeton, playing marbles for keeps and cutting kite strings. As a child, Lucy was friendly with several of the Poplar Springs boys and enjoyed flying kites with them. She noted that kites in those days were split bamboo frames with bright paper wings, rag tails and balls of string.

Templeton added, "I was never any good at games, but I excelled at flying kites. I could get my kite up when others flopped, and usually to a greater height than any of the others." After getting their kites up, the children sat in the grass and talked, watching their kites soar, testing the lines and sending messages up.

Isabel White, later Mrs. J. Ernest Briscoe, recalled that, during her Elmwood Park childhood, the Elmwood neighborhood stopped at Bertrand Street, where the Poplar Springs neighborhood began. And even though the first 1850s streets and houses of Shieldstown between First Creek and Bertrand were the core streets and houses of Elmwood Park, residents of Elmwood Park's 1880s Victorians did not consider themselves part of Shieldstown at all—Shieldstown was what they called Poplar Springs.

Another *Country Calendar* reader, a Poplar Springs resident, name not given, recalled in 1948 that the Park City he knew was called Shieldstown in the old days, not Elmwood. He had attended the Belleview School on Howard Street, a few blocks from the later Park-Lowry School. He remembered, "I also learned to swim in First Creek below the Knoxville Knitting Mills, which area was then known as White's Pasture. The creek would be warm and colored red, blue, or black, depending on the dye they were using that day at the mills."

Victorian farmhouse, 114 Bertrand Street, Poplar Springs. *Photo by Margery W. Bensey.*

Craftsman bungalow, 120 Keller Street, Poplar Springs. *Photo by Kiernan W. Bensey.*

Craftsman bungalow, 1940 McCalla Avenue, Poplar Springs. *Photo by Kiernan W. Bensey.*

A few older houses were still standing in Poplar Springs in the 1990s after I moved into the neighborhood, on Linden, Magnolia and East Fifth Avenues, between Bertrand and Olive Streets: small cottages with old-fashioned arches and posts and farmhouses with decorative trim, alongside foursquares and bungalows from a later era.

Early residents of Poplar Springs included Moses White, son of Knoxville's founder, James White, the original owner of the farmland; Joseph Bell, the farmer who bought some of the Moses White land; and Preston Blang, an Irishman, who married a Bell daughter and subdivided the land further.

Later Poplar Springs families included Brooks, Burnett, Day, Eaton, Frye, Lusby, McClung, Moore, Pickell and Woods families. In the 1880s, the Burnett and Lusby families lived up and down Bertrand Street, large families whose ancestors had owned farmland in the 1860s and whose menfolk worked as brick masons, paperhangers, blacksmiths, wagon drivers and day laborers.

East End

The East End Addition, with its elegant residences, was developed in 1886 on the site of the old fairgrounds where the Confederate army mustered and trained in the early years of the Civil War.

A Knoxville *Chronicle* article in July 1886 noted that fourteen elegant residences had already been built at East End, with more under construction, and in March 1890, an article reported that the developers were holding an auction of lots. The East End Addition was located south of the Rutledge Pike extension of Bell Avenue (McCalla), "at the head of the Mabry and Bell street car line" and "where the electric street car line runs through the center of the property on its route to Beaman Lake." William Rule's *History of Knoxville* placed the mustering grounds and the subdivision "at the southeast corner of the state fair grounds, the eastern extension of Nelson Street (Bethel), parts of which are now known as Orange Street." Two 1824 maps, the Knoxville City Engineer's ward map and the Sanborn fire insurance map, show East End and its streets.

Magnolia Café, 2405 Magnolia Avenue, Cold Springs. *Photo by Kiernan W. Bensey*.

American Foursquare, 2445 Magnolia Avenue, Cold Springs. *Photo by Kiernan W. Bensey.*

American Foursquare, 2455 Magnolia Avenue, Cold Springs. *Photo by Kiernan W. Bensey.*

The western half of the East End Addition was formed around Nelson Circle, centered between the Rutledge Pike extension of Bell Avenue on the north, Orange Avenue (today's Ulster Street) on the south, Chestnut Street on the east and Bell Street (now Ben Hur) on the west. The circle was crossed by Parham Street north to south and Louise Avenue east to west. Nelson Circle was designed with twelve radiating properties, though it does not appear that all of them were developed. In recent years, the small circle has become empty and weedy, and today it is no longer recognizable as a circle. Around its perimeter are twentieth-century Louise Avenue residences on the east and the parking lot of St. Paul's Baptist Church and the backside of the Five Points shopping center on the west.

The eastern half of the East End Addition was centered between Rutledge Pike on the north, Chestnut Street on the west, Cherry Street on the east and a crescent-shaped street uniting Chestnut and Cherry in a curve to the south. The area was trisected by Louise, Wilson and Selma. In the center of Louise, the street widened to create Nelson Place. Between Wilson and Selma, Chestnut Street ended at Union Square, with ten properties lined up along the east side of the square, facing west. The

Brown brick Victorian, 2509 Parkview Avenue, Cold Springs. *Photo by Margery W. Bensey.*

Craftsman bungalow, 813 Biddle Street, Biddle Heights. *Photo by Kiernan W. Bensey.*

lower end of Cherry at this point was called The Corso. Below Selma, Crescent Street formed a curve of eighteen properties facing south between Union Square and The Corso; on the south side of Crescent, fifteen properties faced north.

All of the "elegant residences" built in East End in the 1880s and 1890s are gone. A few turn-of-the century American Foursquares and earlier Victorians still stand in the East End area, just outside the original boundaries of the addition. A large brick Victorian with white Ionic pillars on brick piers still stands a block to the north at 2909 Parkview, perhaps an example of what an East End house was like. Two great brown brick American Foursquares at 2445 and 2455 Magnolia, on the northwest corner of Chestnut, may have been later East End houses, circa 1900—outside the addition, but fitting the period and the architecture of the neighborhood. In the same block is an American Foursquare with decorative corbels at 2405 Magnolia, preserved as the Magnolia Cafe. A brick Craftsman with white Ionic pillars on brick piers at the corner of Biddle and Chestnut, south of East End, may be another example of what an East End house was like.

Victorian replica houses, "The Corso," East End. *Photo by Kiernan W. Bensey.*

Today these sections of Chestnut and Cherry are populated with small modern houses ranging from simple 1930s cottages to present-day historic-design, energy-efficient modern cottages and bungalows. On Louise, Wilson and Selma are a few turn-of-the-century farmhouses and bungalows, but no elegant residences of the Victorian era. Union Square is now a playground, recently renamed in honor of athlete Paul Hogue who grew up in the neighborhood in the 1940s and 1950s and went on to play basketball for the New York Knicks and Baltimore Bullets.

EDGEWOOD

During the development of Elmwood Park and Poplar Springs throughout the 1850s through the 1880s, the area to the north that was to become known as Edgewood was rural and sparsely settled. Orlando Poe's 1863–1864 topographical map of the area shows only hills, fields and woods. White's Field, today's Caswell Park, was the northern

Haworth-Cash house, 1712 Washington Avenue, Edgewood, 1889. Barber House Design No. 3 from *The Cottage Souvenir, No. 1*. *Photo by Margery W. Bensey.*

section of Elmwood Park, and Edgewood developed north of this field, extending from White's Creek, or First Creek, on the west to Boruff Street on the east.

The Edgewood Land and Improvement Company was established by about 1890 by J.C. White, a descendant of Knoxville's founder, James White, who began constructing houses in the Edgewood subdivision just north of Elmwood Park and Poplar Springs. White partnered with George Franklin Barber, an area resident and architect since 1888, who was becoming well known as a mail-order architect. The Edgewood subdivision extended from the 1500 blocks of Glenwood, Washington, Jefferson and Woodbine to the 1800 blocks. The slanted eastern boundary was near Boruff Street; the western boundary was First Creek and Pratt Street Park, past Sixth Avenue, outside the eventual city limits of Park City.

The area has one of the highest concentrations of Barber-designed houses in the nation. Most of the Barber house designs in the Knoxville area are in Edgewood, and most of the Barber houses in Edgewood

Haworth-Ireland house, 1724 Washington Avenue, Edgewood, 1889. Barber House Design No. 35 from *The Cottage Souvenir, No. 2*. *Photo by Kiernan W. Bensey.*

Queen Anne Victorian, 1802 Washington Avenue, Edgewood, 1895. *Photo by Margery W. Bensey.*

Queen Anne Victorian, 1806 Washington Avenue, Edgewood. *Photo by Margery W. Bensey.*

Barber house, 1701 Glenwood Avenue, Edgewood. George F. Barber's last home, 1913–1915, being restored by current owners. *Photo by Margery W. Bensey.*

are on Washington Avenue. Some of the large Victorian, Queen Anne and Eastlake houses with definite or probable Barber designs have been identified on Washington and Jefferson Avenues and elsewhere in Park City. The Barber-designed residences of George F. Barber, his brother and partner Manley DeWitt Barber and his partner J.C. White still stand today at 1635 and 1701 Washington Avenue and 1701 Glenwood.

Hazen Hill

Throughout the 1890s, while J.C. White and George F. Barber were building houses in Edgewood, Asa Hazen was developing Hazen Hill to the north and east, also with Victorian, Queen Anne and Eastlake–style houses. Two earlier subdivisions, Elmwood Park, directly south of Edgewood, and Poplar Springs, directly south of Hazen Hill, had been developed throughout the 1850s–1880s and were populated with Victorian houses of all sizes on expansive lawns or near shady woodlands.

Foreman house, 2038 Jefferson Avenue, Hazen Hill. *Photo by Margery W. Bensey.*

A 1924 ward map created by the City of Knoxville Department of Engineering shows the Hazen Hill Addition just north of Poplar Springs, in the 1800–2400 blocks of Glenwood, Washington and Jefferson Avenues. The western boundary began between Boruff and Bertrand, and the eastern boundary ended at Spruce. The curved residential Adams Avenue north of Glenwood was part of this development.

Although Asa Hazen's real estate firm was selling land in the area in the 1890s, and ward maps and insurance maps depict the subdivision lots, many of the houses in this area appear to have been built later—from the 1920s to the 1960s—and some of the Adams Avenue lots are still the wooded hills of Chestnut Ridge. The earlier houses along Washington and Jefferson are part of the Park City Historic District and the Edgewood Historic Overlay.

Notable Hazen Hill residents included the Burwells and Coiles. In 1891, Mary Price and William G. Burwell built the Victorian house at 2320 Jefferson Avenue, still standing. Their daughter Mary was married to Clay Brown Atkin, said to be Knoxville's wealthiest businessman, in

Queen Anne cottage, 2045 Washington Avenue, Hazen Hill. *Photo by Kiernan W. Bensey.*

Burwell house, 2320 Jefferson, Hazen Hill, 1890. *Photo by Kiernan W. Bensey.*

Coile house, 2361 East Fifth Avenue, Hazen Hill. *Photo by Margery W. Bensey.*

1894 and moved to a mansion downtown. The rest of the Burwell family were still living in the Hazen Hill house in 1900.

The Reverend Mr. and Mrs. Alexander J. Coile lived with their family at 2361 East Fifth Avenue on the northeast corner of Olive Street, in the 1890s, a Barber-designed house. The 1894 *Knoxville Blue Book* places them at this Fifth Avenue address. The Reverend Mr. Coile was pastor of the Park City Presbyterian Church, located two blocks south of his house on the corner of Linden Avenue and Olive Street.

COLD SPRINGS

Just east of Poplar Springs is Cold Springs, extending from Olive Street east to Summer Street (Milligan) and from Woodbine Avenue south to Tarleton.

The Cold Springs Addition was once Cold Springs Farm, home of Robert Houston, senator, secretary of state and first sheriff of Knox County, who owned land in the central section of Park City from the

1790s until the 1830s. Houston received the land for his service in the Battle of King's Mountain, as did other early settlers in the area. He is said by some historians to have built the brown brick estate house and stone spring houses still standing today within wrought-iron fences at 2639 Rutledge Pike, today's Dr. Martin Luther King Jr. Boulevard, likely the oldest structures in Park City.

At some point following Houston's death in 1834, the estate house and land were purchased by Joseph A. Mabry Jr., prominent citizen, stock raiser and landowner, likely by 1840, and it is possible that he added to the existing structure or built a new one. He and his family lived on the Cold Springs property until 1858, when Mabry built another house at 1711 Dandridge Pike in the town of Mountain View on a bluff overlooking Park City. That house, occupied by the Mabry-Hazen family for over 125 years, is preserved today as a museum. The Mabrys kept the wooded, secluded Cold Springs Farm in the family for some years as a summer home.

Around 1900, the Cold Springs Farm estate house was sold and became the Mount Rest Home for elderly ladies. The estate served in

Orange brick house, 2501 McCalla Avenue, Cold Springs. *Photo by Kiernan W. Bensey.*

Gray stone house, 750 Hembree, Cold Springs. *Photo by Margery W. Bensey.*

that capacity for many years and has a similar use today. The farmland was divided and sold in standard 50- by 150-foot lots as part of the Cold Springs Addition.

Styles include 1920s Craftsman Bungalows, 1930s cottages with charming details, small plain tract houses from the 1940s and 1950s, modern ranch-style homes from the 1960s and Tudor styles of stone or brick from every decade.

One of the more attractive Craftsman Bungalows, at 2500 Parkview, was home to actress Patricia Neal during her childhood and then became the home of prominent physician Dr. Lee L. Williams and his family. The house is still in the family, home of Dr. Williams's daughter Rosalyn Williams Poole.

Across from the Neal-Williams house, at 2460 Parkview, the southwest corner of Parkview and Chestnut, is the old Park City Methodist Episcopal Church. The building also was home to the congregation of the Bethel African Methodist Episcopal congregation. At the western edge of Cold Springs, on the southwest corner of Linden and Olive, is the old Park City

Neal-Williams house, Craftsman bungalow, 2500 Parkview Avenue, Cold Springs. Actress Patricia Neal lived in this house as a child. It was then owned for many years by prominent physician Dr. Lee L. Williams. Still in the family, the house now belongs to Rosalyn Williams Poole. *Photo by Margery W. Bensey.*

Park City Methodist Church, 2460 Parkview, Cold Springs. *Photo by Margery W. Bensey.*

Park City Presbyterian Church, 2150 Linden Avenue, Cold Springs. *Photo by Margery W. Bensey.*

Presbyterian Church, a Barber design built in 1891. That congregation once worshiped at the Bell Avenue Presbyterian Church on Bell Avenue (McCalla) and Bertrand. Park City Presbyterian's stained-glass windows are said to be from the older Bell Avenue Presbyterian.

LAKE PARK SPRINGS

Just east of Cold Springs is Lake Park Springs, extending from Milligan Street east to Chilhowee Park and from Woodbine Avenue south to old Rutledge Pike, today's Dr. Martin Luther King Jr. Boulevard.

The Lake Park Springs Addition was once part of the farm of Alexander McMillan, who owned land in the eastern section of Park City from the 1790s until the 1870s. McMillan received the land for his service in the Battle of King's Mountain, as did other early settlers in the area. He built his white clapboard estate house in 1787 eight miles to the east at Wooddale, still standing today behind a gate at

Gray stone house, Woodbine Avenue, Lake Park Springs. *Photo by Margery W. Bensey.*

7703 Strawberry Plains Pike, likely the oldest house built on property extending into Park City.

The McMillan land in the Lake Park Springs area was purchased by Fernando Cortez Beaman in 1876. He and his family lived on the Lake Park Springs property until his son Clarence Beaman built a house in the new Lake Park Springs subdivision on Magnolia Avenue and Castle Street in Park City. That house, occupied by the large Beaman family, is no longer standing. The Beamans kept their house on Beaman Lake as a summer home.

Around 1900, much of the Lake Park Springs farmland was divided and sold in standard 50- by 150-foot lots as part of the Lake Park Springs Addition development. The housing includes Craftsman Bungalows, American Foursquares, large rambling homes with Eastlake features and small Tudor styles with archways of stone or brick.

Mary Costa, the well-known opera singer, lived in Lake Park Springs as a child, in the Aston Apartments at 2736 Magnolia Avenue and in

Gray Craftsman bungalow, 3201 East Fifth Avenue, Lake Park Springs. *Photo by Margery W. Bensey.*

Blue Craftsman bungalow, 2701 East Fifth Avenue, Lake Park Springs, circa 1920. *Photo by Margery W. Bensey.*

Pickell house, 2760 Magnolia Avenue, Lake Park Springs. *Photo by Kiernan W. Bensey.*

a Cape Cod–style house at 3016 (now 3024) East Fifth Avenue. Mary is remembered by the Pickell sisters—Edith, Helen and Eleanor—who lived across the street in a Craftsman Bungalow at 3017 (now 3037) East Fifth Avenue in the 1940s. Another Pickell family house was located at 2760 Magnolia.

One of the most attractive Craftsman Bungalows in Lake Park Springs, at 3117 East Fifth Avenue, pictured, was built in the early 1900s on a block that came to be known as "Parsons' Row." The builder was James B. Martin, a manager for the Postal Telephone and Telegraph Company. Martin purchased three standard 50- by 150-foot lots in the 3100 block of East Fifth Avenue and built two houses, centering each on a 75- by 150-foot lot. Thus the house at 3107 East Fifth stands on one half of the triple lot and the house at 3117 East Fifth on the other half.

According to Nancy Mott, resident of Parson's Row, records show that Martin was living at 3107 East Fifth Avenue in 1913 but later sold the house to Church Street United Methodist Church for their parsonage. The house at 3117 East Fifth was purchased by Third Presbyterian

Art Deco Craftsman bungalow, Parson's Row, 3117 East Fifth Avenue, Lake Park Springs. *Photo by Margery W. Bensey.*

Cherry Park-In, 2601 Magnolia Avenue, Lake Park Springs. All the East High kids got their burgers and fries at this drive-in, run by Carolyn Needham's father. *Photo courtesy of Carolyn Needham Ellis.*

Church, also on East Fifth, and sometimes known as Fifth Avenue Presbyterian, for use as their parsonage. And thus the block became known as "Parson's Row."

At the edges of this neighborhood, Chilhowee Park and downtown Park City have thrived for over a century.

Chapter 7
GEORGE BARBER, VICTORIAN ARCHITECT

The Park City Historic District is said to have the highest concentration of Victorian houses in the nation designed by George W. Barber, one of the era's best-known and most-noted architects. At this writing, two dozen definite Barber-designed houses have been identified in Park City, with many houses in the area resembling Barber designs.

George Barber the Architect

George Barber, the Victorian era's most prolific mail-order architect, began his career in DeKalb, Illinois, creating mail-order house plans. His designs included Chalet, Eastlake, Bungalow, Queen Anne, Colonial Revival and Dutch Colonial styles.

Barber moved to the southern mountains for his health, arrived in Knoxville in 1888, and went into business with various associates, first as Barber and Parmelee and then as Barber and Klintz. In 1896, he partnered with J.C. White, a descendant of Knoxville's founder, who had already established the Edgewood Land and Improvement Company to build Victorian houses primarily in a subdivision that became known as Edgewood, though these houses appear throughout Park City.

Manley DeWitt Barber, a well-known draftsman, builder and contractor, moved to Knoxville in 1903 and joined his brother George in business. Manley was better known for his collection of shells and fossils, said to have been the largest in the United States. New specimens he found were sent to the Smithsonian Institution to be named, with three specimens named after Manley.

By the early 1900s, George Barber's architectural firm was the largest in the state. His son Charles Barber and nephew West Barber, both of whom grew up in Park City, went on to design houses and buildings for their firm Barber and McMurry.

Barber Family Houses

George Barber designed and resided in several Edgewood Park houses. The house at 1635 Washington Avenue, where he lived with his family from 1889 until 1895, is still standing, Design No. 60 from *The Cottage*

Barber-Philippi house, 1635 Washington Avenue, Edgewood, 1889. Barber House Design No. 60 from *The Cottage Souvenir, No. 2*. Two Barber brothers lived here: George F. Barber and family (1889–1895) and Manley D. Barber and family (1903–1914). *Photo by Margery W. Bensey.*

Souvenir, No.2. Barber lived there with his wife, Laura, and children Charles, George and Laura.

Manley Barber, his wife, Sarah, and their children Alice, Guy, West and Laura lived at 1635 Washington from 1903 until 1914. Manley Barber owned the Dutch Colonial across the street at 1620 Washington from 1905 until 1911, though he and his family did not live there. It's Design No. A71, *Keith's Magazine*, January 1905, a variation of Design No. 239, *Modern Dwellings*, built in 1905.

The Barber-designed home of J.C. White still stands at 1701 Washington Avenue, Design No. 60, *The Cottage Souvenir, No. 2*, built as a Victorian but remodeled as a Craftsman following a fire.

Another George Barber family house, Rosemont, no longer standing, is thought to have been located at 1715 Washington Avenue, the address where George Barber and his family lived in 1910. The architect lived at 1701 Glenwood at the end of his life, from 1913 until 1915, in a Colonial Revival style still standing in the foothills of Chestnut Ridge at the end of Monroe Street. The house interior has Barber characteristics and is likely his design, though no plans for it have as yet been discovered.

BARBER PUBLICATIONS

Barber's catalogs included *The Cottage Souvenir* (1891), with eighteen plans; *The Cottage Souvenir No. 2* (1892), with seventy plans; *New Model Dwellings* (1894); and *Artistic Homes* (1895). His magazines were *Art in Architecture* (two issues, 1902–1903); *Modern Dwellings* (nine issues, 1898–1907); and the monthly *American Homes* (six years).

After Barber's death, his work was carried on throughout the nation. Sears, Roebuck and Company and Montgomery Ward and Company were offering prefabricated houses by mail order.

Today Barber's design catalogs are available in the McClung Collection in the East Tennessee History Center in downtown Knoxville and on the collection's website. *Modern Dwellings* can viewed online through Google Books as well.

Some of Barber's designs from *The Cottage Souvenir, No. 2* and *Modern Dwellings* have been reproduced in *Victorian Cottage Architecture: An American*

Catalog of Designs (Dover Books, 2004) and *Turn-of-the-Century Houses: Elevations and Floor Plans* (Dover Books, 2008).

In recent years, Barber's work has been receiving attention from two Barber design researchers, Dr. Michael Tomlan at Cornell University, who wrote the introductions for the reproductions, and the late Dr. Michael Alcorn, formerly of the University of Nevada. Photographs of Barber houses across the nation have been available in exhibits and publications. Barber house enthusiasts have an online discussion site, Merry Meeting.

Definite and Probable Barber Designs

Barber-designed houses in various styles were built on Glenwood, Washington, Jefferson and Woodbine Avenues in the Edgewood and Hazen Hill subdivisions. And possible Barber house designs appear on East Fifth, Magnolia, Linden, Parkview, McCalla and Vine Avenues in the Elmwood Park, Poplar Springs, Cold Springs and Lake Park Springs subdivisions.

Sanders-Arnett-Terry house, 1626 Washington Avenue, Edgewood, 1902. *Photo by Margery W. Bensey.*

Deaver-Perry house, 1803 Washington Avenue, Edgewood, 1893. Barber House Design No. 60B from *New Model Dwellings*. *Photo by Margery W. Bensey.*

Houses in Park City with definite or probable Barber designs have been identified by neighborhood residents and historians at 1701 and 1810 Glenwood Avenue; 1614, 1618, 1620, 1635, 1701, 1702, 1704, 1705, 1712, 1724, 1730, 1803, 1804, 1904, 1912, 2331 and 2343 Washington Avenue; 1603, 1640, 1701, 1708, 1731, 2001 and 2039 Jefferson Avenue; and 1501 Woodbine Avenue. These and other houses that show Barber influence are listed below, street by street.

GLENWOOD AVENUE (FORMERLY COLEMAN)

1701 Glenwood: A likely Barber design, unidentified; George W. Barber's last residence from 1913 to 1915 and his home at the time of his death.
1705 Glenwood: Queen Anne cottage with features similar to Design No. 581, *Art in Architecture*, and No. 265, *Modern Dwellings*.
1810 Glenwood: Design No. 9, *The Cottage Souvenir, No. 2*, built 1889.
1812 Glenwood: Queen Anne cottage with features similar to Design No. 581, *Art in Architecture*, and No. 265, *Modern Dwellings*.

Washington Avenue (Also Highland and Waverly)

1614 Washington: Design No. 266, *Modern Dwellings*, and Design No. 600, *Art in Architecture*, built in 1904.
1618 Washington: Design No. 65B, *New Model Dwellings*, built 1890.
1620 Washington: Dutch Colonial, Design No. A71, *Keith's Magazine*, (January 1905); variation of Design No. 239, *Modern Dwellings*, built 1905.
1626 Washington: Queen Anne cottage with features similar to Design No. 581, *Art in Architecture* and No. 265, *Modern Dwellings*.
1635 Washington: Design No. 60, *The Cottage Souvenir, No. 2*, built 1889.
1701 Washington: Unidentified Barber design reconstructed after a fire.
1702 Washington: Design No. 43, *The Cottage Souvenir, No. 2*, built 1889.
1704 Washington: Design No. 37B, *New Model Dwellings*.
1705 Washington: Design No. 54, *The Cottage Souvenir, No. 2*.
1712 Washington: Design No. 3, *The Cottage Souvenir, No. 1,* built in 1889.
1724 Washington: Design No. 35, *The Cottage Souvenir, No. 2*.
1730 Washington: Likely Barber design, unidentified, built about 1890.
1801 Washington: Likely Barber design, unidentified.
1802 Washington: Likely Barber design, unidentified, built in 1895.
1803 Washington: Design No. 60B, *New Model Dwellings*.
1804 Washington: Design No. 124, *Cottage Souvenir Revised and Enlarged*
1806 Washington: Resembles Design No. 18, *The Cottage Souvenir, No. 2*.
1904 Washington: Design No. 12, *Cottage Souvenir, No. 2*, modified.
1905 Washington: Likely Barber design, unidentified.
1912 Washington: Design No. 38, *Cottage Souvenir, No. 2*, modified.
2045 Washington: Queen Anne cottage with features similar to Design No. 581, *Art in Architecture*, and No. 265, *Modern Dwellings*.
2331 Washington: Design No. 38, *The Cottage Souvenir, No. 2*, built 1893.
2343 Washington: Design No. 38, *The Cottage Souvenir, No. 2*, built 1893.

JEFFERSON AVENUE (ALSO MICHIGAN)

1603 Jefferson: Design No. 60B, *New Model Dwellings.*
1607 Jefferson: Queen Anne cottage with features similar to Design No. 581, *Art in Architecture*, and No. 265, *Modern Dwellings.*
1616 Jefferson: Queen Anne cottage with features similar to Design No. 581, *Art in Architecture*, and No. 265, *Modern Dwellings.*
1640 Jefferson: Design No. 264, *Modern Dwellings*, built in the 1890s.
1701 Jefferson: Design No. 40, *The Cottage Souvenir, No. 2*, built 1889.
1708 Jefferson: Design No. 39, *The Cottage Souvenir, No. 2*, built 1889.
1730 Jefferson: Queen Anne cottage with turret and other features similar to Design No. 581, *Art in Architecture*, and No. 265, *Modern Dwellings.*
1731 Jefferson: Design No. 39, *The Cottage Souvenir, No. 2*, built 1889.
2001 Jefferson: Design No. 804 and 806, *Modern American Homes.*
2021 Jefferson: Queen Anne cottage with turret and other features similar to Design No. 581, *Art in Architecture*, and No. 265, *Modern Dwellings.*
2039 Jefferson: Design No. 125, *Cottage Souvenir Revised and Enlarged*
2041 Jefferson: Likely Barber design, unidentified.
2320 Jefferson: Resembles Design No. 21, *The Cottage Souvenir, No. 2.*
2448 Jefferson: Resembles Design No. 16, *The Cottage Souvenir, No. 2.*
2524 Jefferson: Similar features to Barber designs, unidentified.
2536 Jefferson: Resembles Design No. 18, *The Cottage Souvenir, No. 2.*
2537 Jefferson: Resembles Design No. 18, *The Cottage Souvenir, No. 2.*

WOODBINE AVENUE (ALSO MADISON)

1501 Woodbine: Design No. 9, *The Cottage Souvenir, No. 2.*
1535 Woodbine: Resembles Design No. 21, *The Cottage Souvenir, No. 2.*
2306 Woodbine: Resembles Design No. 16, *The Cottage Souvenir, No. 2.*
2346 Woodbine: Resembles Design No. 16, *The Cottage Souvenir, No. 2.*
2358 Woodbine: Resembles Design No. 16, *The Cottage Souvenir, No. 2.*
2360 Woodbine: Dutch Colonial with features similar to Design No. 19 and No. 239, *Modern Dwellings*, and No. 551, *Art and Architecture.*

2449 Woodbine: Resembles Design No. 18, *The Cottage Souvenir, No. 2.*
2460 Woodbine: Resembles Design No. 18, *The Cottage Souvenir, No. 2.*
2644 Woodbine: Resembles Design No. 18, *The Cottage Souvenir, No. 2.*

East Fifth Avenue (Formerly Pavel Street)

1702 East Fifth: Resembles Design No. 21 and 27, *The Cottage Souvenir, No. 2*, modified, built 1909.
2037 East Fifth: Queen Anne cottage with features similar to Design No. 581, *Art in Architecture*, and No. 265, *Modern Dwellings.*
2073 East Fifth: Queen Anne cottage with features similar to Design No. 581, *Art in Architecture*, and No. 265, *Modern Dwellings.*
2351 East Fifth: Similar features to Barber designs, unidentified.
2352 East Fifth: Similar features to Barber designs, unidentified.
2361 East Fifth: Resembles Design No. 15, *The Cottage Souvenir, No. 2.*
2413 East Fifth: Resembles Design No. 15, *The Cottage Souvenir, No. 2.*
2417 East Fifth: Queen Anne cottage with features similar to Design No. 581, *Art in Architecture*, and No. 265, *Modern Dwellings.*
2439 East Fifth: Queen Anne cottage with features similar to Design No. 581, *Art in Architecture*, and No. 265, *Modern Dwellings.*
2501 East Fifth: Queen Anne cottage with features similar to Design No. 581, *Art in Architecture*, and No. 265, *Modern Dwellings.*

Magnolia Avenue (Formerly Craig Street)

1405 Magnolia: Queen Anne cottage with features similar to Design No. 581, *Art in Architecture*, and No. 265, *Modern Dwellings.*
1407 Magnolia: Queen Anne cottage with features similar to Design No. 581, *Art in Architecture*, and No. 265, *Modern Dwellings.*
2326 Magnolia: Queen Anne cottage with features similar to Design No. 581, *Art in Architecture*, and No. 265, *Modern Dwellings.*
2358 Magnolia: Dutch Colonial with features similar to Design No. 19 and No. 239, *Modern Dwellings*, and No. 551, *Art and Architecture.*

2412 Magnolia: Dutch Colonial, Design No. 551, *Art and Architecture.*
3115 Magnolia: Dutch Colonial with features similar to Design No. 19 and No. 239, *Modern Dwellings*, and No. 551, *Art and Architecture.*

PARKVIEW AVENUE (FORMERLY VIRGINIA AVENUE)

2305 Parkview: Dutch Colonial with features similar to Design No. 19 and No. 239, *Modern Dwellings*, and No. 551, *Art and Architecture.*
2306 Parkview: Dutch Colonial with features similar to Design No. 19 and No. 239, *Modern Dwellings*, and No. 551, *Art and Architecture.*
2310 Parkview: Dutch Colonial with features similar to Design No. 19 and No. 239, *Modern Dwellings*, and No. 551, *Art and Architecture.*
2417 Parkview: Resembles Design No. 21 or 27, *The Cottage Souvenir, No. 2.*

LINDEN AVENUE (FORMERLY HOWARD)

2111 Linden: Queen Anne cottage with features similar to Design No. 581, *Art in Architecture*, and No. 265, *Modern Dwellings.*
2115 Linden: Queen Anne cottage with features similar to Design No. 581, *Art in Architecture*, and No. 265, *Modern Dwellings*
2307 Linden: Possible Design No. 21 or 27, *The Cottage Souvenir, No. 2.*
2343 Linden: Queen Anne cottage with features similar to Design No. 581, *Art in Architecture*, and No. 265, *Modern Dwellings.*

MCCALLA AVENUE (ALSO BELL AVENUE, JACKSON AVENUE, RUTLEDGE PIKE)

2243 McCalla: Queen Anne cottage with features similar to Design No. 581, *Art in Architecture*, and No. 265, *Modern Dwellings.*
2247 McCalla: Brick residence with features similar to Design No. 29, *The Cottage Souvenir, No. 2.*

Dr. Martin Luther King Jr. Boulevard (Mabry Street, Vine Street, Ramsey Ferry Road)

2217 MLK: Queen Anne cottage with features similar to Design No. 581, *Art in Architecture*, and No. 265, *Modern Dwellings*.
2221 MLK: Queen Anne cottage with features similar to Design No. 581, *Art in Architecture*, and No. 265, *Modern Dwellings*.
2805 MLK: Resembles Design No. 30 in *The Cottage Souvenir, No. 2*.
2815 MLK: Queen Anne cottage with features similar to Design No. 581, *Art in Architecture*, and No. 265, *Modern Dwellings*.
2826 MLK: Queen Anne cottage with features similar to Design No. 581, *Art in Architecture*, and No. 265, *Modern Dwellings*.
2828 MLK: Queen Anne cottage with features similar to Design No. 581, *Art in Architecture*, and No. 265, *Modern Dwellings*.
3140 MLK: Resembles Design No. 21 or 27, *The Cottage Souvenir, No. 2*.
3210 MLK: Resembles designs in *The Cottage Souvenir, No. 2*.
3316 MLK: Resembles Design No. 18 in *The Cottage Souvenir, No. 2*.
3601 MLK: Queen Anne cottage with features similar to Design No. 581, *Art in Architecture*, and No. 265, *Modern Dwellings*.
3605 MLK: Queen Anne cottage with features similar to Design No. 581, *Art in Architecture*, and No. 265, *Modern Dwellings*.
3700 MLK: Queen Anne cottage with features similar to Design No. 581, *Art in Architecture*, and No. 265, *Modern Dwellings*.

Chapter 8

PARK CITY'S INCORPORATION

The Birthplace of Park City

After the turn of the century, the seven residential areas that developed around Eastport and Shieldstown were incorporated as the town of Park City: Elmwood Park, Poplar Springs, East End, Edgewood, Hazen Hill, Cold Springs and Lake Park Springs. Park City was incorporated on February 19, 1907, when its charter was read and signed at Belleview Presbyterian Church on the corner of Belleview Avenue (West Fifth) and Williams Street in North Knoxville.

Present were William R. Johnson, the new mayor; John J. Graham, recorder; James Henry Welcker, attorney and recipient of the charter; William Knabe, magistrate and administrator of oaths; and eight aldermen. The aldermen were William A. Davis, John M. Dailey Jr., Thomas Dooley, Christopher C. Cruze, Albert A. Greenwood, Gilson L. Moore, George L. Price and William H. Underwood.

Park City's Mayors

William R. Johnson, of 2656 Magnolia Avenue, was Park City's first mayor. He was fifty years old and had been married seven years to Della Hennessey when he became the first mayor of Park City on February 19,

Cruze house, 2023 Washington Avenue, Edgewood, 1893. Christopher Cruze, one of the founders of Park City, lived here with his family. *Photo by Kiernan W. Bensey.*

1907. He was reelected on May 19, 1908, to serve another two years. At the time, he was in business as a cigar manufacturer; later, he was in real estate. The Johnsons lived on a block of brick and stone mansions, some of which still stand today near Magnolia Methodist Church, though the mayor's manse is gone.

William A. Davis, of 2707 East Fifth Avenue, was Park City's last mayor. He was forty-five and married twenty-two years when Park City was incorporated, working as an agent, claims adjustor and freight manager for the Southern Railway. As alderman, he served the eighth district of Park City and headed the new business committee. He was married to Cora M. Pope, sister of nurseryman Arthur Pope. Their children were Earl, nineteen; Wilford, sixteen; Kenneth, fourteen; Mabel, twelve; Jane, ten; and Edith, seven. Davis was serving as mayor of Park City in 1917 when the town was incorporated by Knoxville. The mayor's manse once stood among the large craftsman houses with wood siding and wood shingles near Chilhowee Park.

Park City's First Recorder

John J. Graham, of 2344 Magnolia Avenue, was chosen as city recorder for the new city. At the time of incorporation, Graham, thirty-nine, was a post office cashier. He and his wife, Emma, married twenty years, were the parents of Benjamin, eleven; James, nine; Mary, six; Melinda, four; Joseph, two; and baby Charles.

Recipient of the Park City Charter

The Honorable James Henry Welcker, fifty-two and living at 1502 Linden (Chilhowee) Avenue, was a partner with Sansom, Welcker and Parker, attorneys, when he received the Park City charter; later, he served as judge. He and his wife, Dixie, were the parents of four sons.

Administrator of Oaths

The Honorable William Knabe, forty, lived at 701 West Cumberland Avenue. As notary, magistrate and justice of the peace, he had an office at 313 West Clinch Avenue, Knoxville. He administered the oaths of office for the mayor and nine alderman on the day of Park City's formation. At the time, Knabe and his wife, Lilla, were the parents of two sons: Karl, fifteen, and Earl, eleven.

Park City's 1907 Aldermen

John M. Dailey Jr., of 1421 Magnolia Avenue, was with the Knoxville City Mills, also known as Standard Knitting Mills, when Park City was incorporated that year. Dailey served the third ward as alderman and chaired a business committee. That year, he was thirty-nine and married seventeen years; he and his wife, Margaret, had two children: Ruth, eight, and Hale, six.

Thomas Dooley, of 2522 Virginia (Parkview) Avenue, was fifty-two and married twenty-five years when he was appointed alderman. He was a Southern Railway conductor and a brother of Southern Railway conductor Clinton Dooley, forty-six, who lived nearby at 2541 Virginia Avenue. As alderman, Thomas Dooley served the city-at-large and headed the fire and police committee. He and his wife, Dora, were the parents of Mabel, twenty-four, a high school teacher; Caroline, twenty-one; Robert, eighteen, a grocery shipping clerk; Leslie, fourteen; and Thomas, eleven.

Christopher C. Cruze, 2023 Washington Avenue, was vice-president of McClung, Buffet and Buckwell in 1900 and was a retail merchant with his own business, Cruze, Sterling and Company by 1907. Cruze was forty years of age and married twenty years when he was elected alderman for the fourth ward of Park City, heading one of the town committees. In later years, Cruze Street in Park City, a few blocks from his home, was named for his family. He and his wife, Helena, were the parents of Elizabeth, fifteen, and Frederick, three.

Albert A. Greenwood, of 1731 Washington Avenue, was forty-eight, married twenty years and had his own wallpaper business, A. Greenwood and Company, at 515 South Gay Street, Knoxville. As alderman, Greenwood served the first ward and headed the lighting committee. He and his wife, Anna, had two daughters: Alberta, eighteen, and Grace, sixteen.

Gilson L. Moore, of 1227 Glenwood Avenue, was thirty-seven and married eight years, with his own company, the Moore Furniture Company. As alderman, Moore served the sixth ward and headed the sanitary committee. When he took office, he and his wife, Harriet, were the parents of four sons and a daughter: Howard, seven; Gladys, six; Gilson, four; Noble, two; and baby Owen. By 1910, they had two more daughters: Margaret and Hazel.

George L. Price, of Fountain Avenue, forty-seven and married twenty-two years, was a dry goods wholesale merchant with D.B. Briscoe Brothers and Company, located at 326–328 South Gay Street, Knoxville. As alderman, Price served the fifth ward and headed the finance committee. He and his wife, Anna, had no children but made a home for their nephew Albert Kincade, eleven.

William H. Underwood, of 2306 Linden Avenue, was forty-one and married twelve years at the time of his appointment. He ran a gentleman's clothing and furnishing business, Sullivan and Underwood,

Park City Library, 2501 Magnolia Avenue, Cold Springs. *Photo by Margery W. Bensey.*

located at 321 South Gay Street, Knoxville. As alderman, Underwood served the fourth ward and headed the streets committee. He and his wife, Clara, were the parents of Trula, eleven; Floyd, nine; William, four; and baby Helen.

Chapter 9

PARK CITY FAMILIES

In this chapter, and in earlier chapters, are biographies of selected Park City residents from the author's genealogies on area families and longer works-in-progress, *Shieldstown Families* and *Shieldstown Streets*. *Shieldstown Families* offers histories of over one hundred area families, and *Shieldstown Streets* lists their homes by address in a walking tour format. Below are histories of twenty area families from old Shieldstown, its Victorian subdivisions or the incorporated town of Park City.

Allen, Mabry and Bell Streets, Elmwood Park

Mr. and Mrs. John Allen lived on the north side of Mabry Street at the corner of Bell Street, today a curve of Old Vine Avenue intersecting with Bell in a brick apartment complex below Summit Hill Drive. The Allen house, no longer there, stood in the 1880s at the north end of Elmwood Park in the shadow of Fort Huntington-Smith across the road at the crest of Temperance Hill.

John Allen, a farmer and laborer, married Sophia Alexander in Knox County in 1828, when he was twenty-three and she was twenty-four, and they had seven children born between 1830 and 1848: Margaret, Nancy, Priscilla, Jane, Walker, Isabella and Calvin.

Nellie Brooks grew up at 1802 East Fifth Avenue in Poplar Springs. She enlisted in the U.S. Army in 1917, then married Joseph W. Frye in 1918 and was the mother of a large Park City family. *Photo courtesy of J.W. Frye.*

The area's census records follow the Allens through their lives, with John laboring and farming, Sophia keeping house and their grown children and grandchildren living with them or near them. In 1860, they were in their fifties, married over thirty years. Older daughters Margaret and Jane were married and living away from home. With the parents were Nancy and Priscilla, in their twenties; Walker, fifteen; and Calvin, eleven. Isabella, twelve, was elsewhere at the time of the census.

By 1870, in their sixties, married over forty years, the Allens were living in District 1, Knox County, where John was farming six hundred acres. Of the older daughters in their thirties, Margaret was back, her maiden named resumed, Nancy was still living at home and Priscilla was now gone. In their twenties, Walker was still living at home, Isabella was again living elsewhere and Calvin was likely deceased. Jane Allen Gibbs was widowed, remarried to Joseph G. Caldwell and living elsewhere, but her son John C. Gibbs, six, was with his Allen grandparents.

In 1880, Sophia and John Allen, in their seventies, married more than fifty years, were now living in the Elmwood Park neighborhood of Shieldstown, on the north side of Mabry, one east of Bell, surrounded by family. John Allen's sister Margaret Allen Lawson, widow of Charles Lawson, made her home with them. Also part of the household were the Allens' son Walker, employed as a boatman; his wife, Caroline N. Rose; and their daughter Alice Walker Allen. Jane Allen Caldwell and her teenage son John Gibbs were living there too, though her husband, Joseph G. Caldwell, was elsewhere.

To the east of the Allen house was the home of their daughter Nancy Allen Tillet; her husband George Tillet, a carpenter; and their children,

James, Joseph, Nancy and Samuel. The children's paternal grandmother, Susan Tillet, in her eighties, lived with them. Their house on Mabry, five east of Bell, stood east of the present-day curve of Old Vine Avenue, on the lawn of a brick apartment complex. One more house to the east, next-door to the Tillets, was the home of the Allens' youngest daughter, Isabella M. Allen, and her husband, James P. Davis, first cousin of the author's great-grandfather.

Black, 1521 Bell Avenue (Jackson, McCalla), Elmwood Park

In 1900, Nancy Freels Black, fifty-five, widow of Samuel Early Black, was living at 1521 Bell Avenue, Elmwood Park, renamed Jackson, later to become McCalla. With her were her three sons Joseph McDaniel Black, thirty; John Black, twenty-eight; and William Freels Black, twenty, who were in business together. Daughters Maria T. Black, twenty-five, and Elisabeth Black, twenty-four, called Betty, were not listed with the family and likely were married and living elsewhere under different names. The Blacks were descendants of Joseph L. Black of Black's Station, who settled Anderson County.

Nancy J. Freels was born in 1845 in Anderson County, the daughter of W.S. Freels. The Freels family were members of the Methodist Episcopal Church South. Samuel Early Black was born March 29, 1840, the son of Elisabeth Early and John Black. He was reared on the family farm with his five younger sisters and brothers and was educated in Anderson County schools and also near Clinton. He worked on the family farm until August 1861, when he enlisted in Company H of the First Tennessee Federal Infantry, in which he served until the organization of the Third Infantry. He was discharged in February 1865 at Nashville and began farming again.

Burwell, 2320 Jefferson Avenue, Hazen Hill

Mary Price and William G. Burwell married in the 1860s and had five children between 1864 and 1878: Elizabeth, Anne, Mary, William and John. Their daughter Elizabeth married John Warrington in about 1884 and lived in Philadelphia for the rest of the 1880s, and then moved to Knoxville in 1891. Her parents came with them and brought their family to Knoxville as well. The Burwells rented a house on East Fifth Avenue while building a house at 2320 Jefferson Avenue in the Hazen Hill area. The family's third daughter, Mary, married wealthy Knoxville businessman Clay Brown Atkin in Knoxville in 1894. The family's first son, William, died in Knoxville in 1895 at age thirty-one. Mary Price Burwell died in November 1896 in Knoxville. William G. Burwell and his son John, twenty-three, appeared in the 1900 census record for Knox County, still living in the Hazen Hill house. William G. Burwell died in February 1905 in Knoxville.

CALDWELL, 1420 LINDEN AVENUE (CHILHOWEE), ELMWOOD PARK

Mr. and Mrs. Thomas M. Caldwell Sr. lived with their family at 1420 Linden Avenue on the southwest corner of Winona Street in the 1880s–1900s. Mrs. Caldwell was the former Miss Jennie Kearsley of Virginia; her two sisters, Mrs. Selden and Mrs. Galyon, lived nearby with their families. Thomas Caldwell and his brother-in-law Andrew Selden ran a grocery together on the east side of Market Square in downtown Knoxville. The 1882 city directory listed Thomas Caldwell in business as a shoemaker. Caldwell and his family lived at the edge of Elmwood Park on the north side of Mabry, two east of Patton Street, but by 1888 they were residing in Elmwood Park.

Many new houses were being built in Elmwood Park in the 1880s, and the Caldwells' may have been one of them. Lucy Curtis Templeton, who grew up a block away at Linden and Myrtle in one of the new Elmwood Park houses recalled the Caldwells as neighbors in her childhood memories and wrote about them in her *Country Calendar* newspaper column. She remembered the Caldwell sons, George, Thomas Jr. and Hugh, and kept in touch with them over the years, so she knew that Hugh Caldwell became mayor of Seattle, which she reported in her column in 1948.

Coile, 2361 East Fifth Avenue, Hazen Hill

The Reverend Mr. and Mrs. Alexander J. Coile lived with their family at 2361 East Fifth Avenue in Hazen Hill, on the northeast corner of Olive Street, in the 1890s. Their house, designed by George Barber, provided a home to a century of Park City families, then was donated by the City of Knoxville to the Parkridge Community Organization in the 1980s for use as a community center.

In the 1890s, Alexander Coile was pastor of Third Presbyterian Church, located two blocks south of his house on the corner of Linden Avenue and Olive Street in Poplar Springs. The Barber-designed church building still stands a few blocks south on Linden Avenue at Olive Street, more recently known as Park City Presbyterian.

The church's stained-glass windows are said to be from the original Bell Avenue Presbyterian Church, established a few blocks southeast on Bell Avenue (later Jackson, then McCalla) at Bertrand Street, in the 1880s. When Bell Avenue Presbyterian changed locations, it became known as Third Presbyterian Church.

Creekmore, 2727 East Fifth Avenue, Lake Park Springs

Louis M. Creekmore lived at 2727 East Fifth with his family in the 1930s. He was from a Kentucky family and married his wife, Dillie, in the early 1900s. Their six children were born between 1909 and 1924: James, Viola, Edwin, Marion, Pollyanna and Thomas. During the years 1910–1920, the Creekmores lived on Fifth Avenue in Jellico, Tennessee; by 1930, they were living on Fifth Avenue in Knoxville, Tennessee. The 1930 *Knox County Census* lists Louis as a barber, age forty-six, with his wife, Dillie, and their children. Pollyanna Creekmore became a well-known librarian and historian with many publications. The house is still standing on the corner of Hembree Street.

CRUZE, 2002 BELL AVENUE (JACKSON, MCCALLA), POPLAR SPRINGS

John W. Cruze was listed in the 1882 *Knoxville City Directory* with his parents, Mr. and Ms. John H. Cruze, and brother Christopher, fifteen, at the northwest corner of Church and Henley in downtown Knoxville. Both brothers worked as clerks in their father's hardware store, J.H. Cruze, located in downtown Knoxville on the east side of State Street, five north of Cumberland, in the 1880s. John W. Cruze spent his life in the business of stoves and tinware, and his family home was located at 2002 Bell Avenue in Poplar Springs, just east of Elmwood Park, both rapidly growing subdivisions in the 1880s. The 1894 *Knoxville Blue Book* and the 1900 *Knoxville Cookbook* both show the Cruzes still living at 2002 Bell Avenue. With them in 1894 is a man named C.P. Cruze, perhaps a grown son, and with them in 1900 is James Cruze, perhaps a widowed relative. Their street was renamed Jackson Avenue by 1900 and McCalla Avenue in later years. The house is no longer standing.

CRUZE, 2023 WASHINGTON AVENUE, HAZEN HILL

Christopher C. Cruze was listed in the 1882 *Knoxville City Directory* living with his parents, Mr. and Mrs. John H. Cruze, and brother John W. Cruze, at the northwest corner of Church and Henley in downtown Knoxville. At the age of fifteen that year, he was working alongside his brother as a clerk in their father's hardware store, J.H. Cruze, located in downtown Knoxville on the east side of State Street, five north of Cumberland, in the 1880s. Christopher C. Cruze married his wife, Helena, in 1887 when he was twenty, and they raised their children at 2023 Washington Avenue, in the Hazen Hill suburb where the town of Park City was developing. Their daughter Elizabeth was born in 1893, the year their house was built, and their son Frederick in 1904. The Cruze house was built in 1893, with Eastlake and Bungalow influences, and is still standing.

Curtis, 1501 and 1502 Linden Avenue (Chilhowee), Elmwood Park

Ida Whitlow and Henry William Curtis married in Lynchburg, Virginia, in about 1875, then moved to Knoxville by 1880, where Henry Curtis had a jewelry shop on Gay Street. They lived in several Elmwood Park locations in the 1880s with their son, Henry, and daughter, Lucy. Lucy Curtis recalled growing up in Elmwood Park and the neighbors around her in childhood memories from about 1888 and wrote about them under the name of Lucy Curtis Templeton in her *Country Calendar* newspaper columns during her fifty-year tenure with the *Knoxville News Sentinel*.

The Curtis family lived in a large house on Mabry Hill in Mountain View, three east of Central, at the edge of Elmwood Park in the early 1880s when Lucy was very young. They then had rooms in the Lamar House in downtown Knoxville during her father's illness, while leasing the Mabry Hill house to another family. Later, Henry Curtis had a cottage built on his Mabry Hill property where the family lived while he continued to recover from his illness and the accompanying financial setback, still leasing the larger house to another family. After recovering his health and wealth, Mr. Curtis built two new houses in the Elmwood Park subdivision.

The house at 1502 Linden Avenue, at the southeast corner of Linden and Winona, was constructed in about 1886, and the Curtises lived there for a year. Lucy recalled playing with friends in the stables, reading in the stable loft, looking out over all of Elmwood Park from the top of the loft and jumping off the roofs of the low coal and tool houses along the backyard fence. The Curtises then sold the house to the Welcker family and built a larger house across the street.

A larger house at 1501 Linden Avenue, at the northeast corner of Linden and Winona, was constructed in about 1887 on a double lot, 1501–1503 Linden, and the Curtis family lived there for two years. The house had oak-paneled walls in the library and dining room and fireplace tiles from the Rookwood pottery in Cincinnati. The builder was named Stephenson, from northern England, and Templeton recalled his pronunciation of the oak paneling he used: "hoak."

In 1957, Templeton reported, the Welcker and Curtis houses were still standing on their corners, seventy years old, but converted to apartments, with outside stairs "sprouting from every direction." The stables were still standing on their alleys, with their rooftop cupolas still in place, long since converted to garages. The coal and tool houses by the backyard fences were long gone. Linden Avenue was now called Chilhowee Avenue, and Howard Street, a parallel street a block away, was now called Linden Avenue.

GALYON, LINDEN AVENUE (CHILHOWEE), ELMWOOOD PARK

Mr. and Mrs. Luther A. Galyon lived with their family at 1411 Linden Avenue, on the north side near Winona Street in the 1880s–1900s. Mrs. Galyon was one of the former Kearsley sisters of Virginia; her two sisters, Mrs. Caldwell and Mrs. Seldon, lived nearby with their families, and their husbands, Thomas Caldwell and Andrew Selden, ran a grocery together on the east side of Market Square in downtown Knoxville. Luther Galyon was listed in the 1882 city directory, working as a carpenter and lumber manufacturer, with a business at 505 Florida Street, living with his family in North Knoxville on Coleman (Glenwood) Avenue near Broadway. By 1888, they had moved to Elmwood Park, where many new houses were being built. The 1894 *Knoxville Blue Book* and the 1900 *Knoxville Cookbook* show the Galyons still at the Linden Avenue address, grown son Eugene Galyon listed with the family in 1900. Their street was renamed Chilhowee Avenue in later years.

JONES, HOWARD (LINDEN) AND BELL STREETS, ELMWOOD PARK

Mr. and Mrs. William H. Jones lived on Howard Street at Bell Street in 1880 when the census taker came to house No. 115. Ellen Jane Compton, fifteen, and William H. Jones, twenty-four, were married in 1853 in Rutledge before the family's move to Shieldstown. Their nine children were born between 1854 and 1879: Columbus, Sarah, Eason, Lillian, Mary Ellen, Caledonia, Christina, Joseph and Jamie.

Ellen Jane Compton, from an old Virginia family transplanted to Tennessee, was the third of six children born to Sarah Fugate and Henry

Compton between 1833 and 1849: Elisabeth, John, Ellen Jane, Virginia, Eliza and William, who died young. The family moved to Grainger County in 1842 and to Knox County in 1853. Their father, Henry Compton, died early in 1854, possibly from a cholera epidemic, leaving behind a widow and five children, ages six through twenty. He is buried in Old Gray Cemetery on Broadway in Knoxville.

After Ellen Compton married William Jones, they made their home on Howard Street at Bell Street, Elmwood Park. When Ellen's older sister Elisabeth married, she lived around the corner on Bell Street at Howard.

The Jones' eldest son, Columbus, married Elisabeth Schaad in 1876 and moved to 1930 Magnolia Avenue, Poplar Springs. Sarah married Christopher Lusby in 1876 and lived on Bertrand Street, Poplar Springs. Eason married Julius Hilton in 1875 and lived in Shieldstown. Lillian married James Showalter in 1881 and moved to Newport, Kentucky. Christina married C.H. Kranstill of Chicago. Jamie married William Rysdon and moved to Waycross, Georgia. Ellen married Andrew Jackson Henry Day in 1884 and lived at 1931 Howard Street, Poplar Springs. He was the son of Anna Elisabeth Davenport and John Henry Day of Spring Street, Poplar Springs, and brother of Isadora Day Black of 1702 East Fifth Avenue, Elmwood Park, the author's home.

Caledonia married Joseph Henry Frye in 1887 and had five children, born between 1888 and 1904: Lillian, Rose Anne, Caledonia, Joseph and Thomas. Their daughter Lillian married Grover Stiles, and their son Joseph W. Frye married Nellie Brooks. Joe and Nellie had eleven children born between 1918 and 1943: Lester, Evelyn, John, William, Elisabeth, J.W., Wanda, Kenneth, Theodore, Glenn and Ronald. Caledonia Jones Frye died in 1918 during the influenza epidemic that killed twenty million people worldwide and is buried at Shieldstown Cemetery in Poplar Springs. Her mother, Ellen Compton Jones, died in 1920 and was buried in Shieldstown Cemetery as well.

Author Lucy Curtis Templeton, who spent her childhood nearby, recalled the Jones family living in the 1400 block of Bell Avenue, on a corner of Winona Street: Miss Lillie, Miss Rosie and, apparently closer to Lucy's age, Carrie and Howard. Templeton returned to the property in 1948 and wrote about it in her column, saying the house was gone, tall weeds covered the yard and there was just one surviving magnolia tree.

LOWRY, 2135 EAST FIFTH AVENUE AND 2117 MAGNOLIA AVENUE, POPLAR SPRINGS

Educators Laura Smith and John D. Lowry made their home at 2135 East Fifth Avenue in 1910 and then 2117 Magnolia Avenue, Poplar Springs, from the 1920s through the 1950s. Laura was a teacher and John was principal of the Mynderse School on Pearl Place and the Park City School on Linden Avenue. He also served as superintendent of schools and vice-president of Knoxville Business College. Park City School was renamed Park-Lowry School in his honor.

MAGBY, BELL STREET, ELMWOOD PARK

One of the more interesting citizens of old Shieldstown, Mrs. Clara Magby, of African heritage, was born in 1780 and was one hundred years old when the census taker visited her home on Bell Street in Elmwood Park. She was listed in the 1880 Shieldstown census as widowed, her grandson's family living with her: William Turk, then thirty-three, working as a stone mason or quarryman; his wife, Dianah Turk, twenty-eight; and their three children, Hubert, six, Alfred, three, and Margaret, one. The 1882 city directory for the Knoxville area listed the family's residence as the west side of Bell Street, seven south of New Street. Next-door were likely more family members: Mary Magby, twenty-five, a black female, widowed; and Addie Craig, a mulatto female, divorced.

MONDAY, 1806 WASHINGTON AVENUE, EDGEWOOD PARK

William Eugene Monday Sr., a real estate proprietor, lived in fashionable Park City with his wife, Mary, and their two children, Mary and Gene, around 1910–1930. Their two-story spindled and shingled Barber-designed house is still standing at 1806 Washington Avenue. By the 1950s, William Eugene Monday Jr. was running several Monday hotels and apartments in downtown Knoxville. Recent holdings owned by William

Eugene Monday III include the Magnolia Apartments at 1701–1703 Magnolia Avenue, the Park Lane Apartments at 1721 East Fifth Avenue and the Monday Apartments at 1801, 1805 and 1809 East Fifth Avenue in Elmwood Park.

Pickell, Poplar Springs, Cold Springs, Lake Park Springs

In the 1880s, J.T. Pickell kept a store at 1901 Howard Street, the northeast corner of Howard and Bertrand. By 1900, he had a branch store at 1618–1620 Vine Avenue in the Five Points area of Cold Springs. J.T. Pickell and his family were living in the yellow brick house at 2760 Magnolia Avenue in Lake Park Springs the year their son Woodward

The Pickell sisters in 1941 with their visiting friends in front of their house at 3037 East Fifth Avenue, Lake Park Springs. *Left to right:* Edith Pickell, twins Eleanor and Helen Pickell, Virginia Bird, Jonathan Howes, Mary Mayne Wilson, Kathryn Bird, Carol Heflin, Jennings Bird and Nancy Howes. *Photo courtesy of Kathryn Kinnard.*

Pickell was a senior in high school, then moved to Sequoyah Hills in the 1920s. Woodward Pickell raised his family in Fort Sanders before he moved them to Lake Park Springs. Helen Huffine and John Woodward Pickell lived at 3017 East Fifth Avenue, later renumbered 3037, with their daughters Edith, Eleanor and Helen.

QUEENER, 1702 EAST FIFTH AVENUE, ELMWOOD PARK

The family of George Washington Queener lived in Park City from the 1890s to the 1920s. Known as Washington Queener, he was born in 1854 in Anderson County, Tennessee, the ninth child and seventh son of Jane Keeney and Grandison Queener and brother of Park City resident Andrew Jackson Queener, born in 1853, who also went by his middle name. The brothers were grandsons of Jacob Queener, who came from Germany in the 1700s and settled south of Big Creek Gap, now Jacksboro, in Campbell County, Tennessee.

In 1877, Washington Queener, twenty-three, and his wife, Martha, fourteen, were married, and became parents of at least two children, Jane Elisabeth, called Jenny, born in 1887, and George Andrew, called Andy, born in 1894. At some point, the family came to Knox County and moved to the Park City area after 1895 but before 1900. That year, Washington Queener was a partner in the Knoxville-area Queener and Bunkley coal and wood business, and his family was living at 1702 East Fifth Avenue, Elmwood Park. The house was a circa 1886 Victorian, inhabited by owners named Campbell in 1886 and Froneberger in 1894. The Queeners moved there between 1895 and 1900 and stayed until 1907.

In 1907, the house burned, and the Queener family moved nine blocks east to 2442 Magnolia Avenue in the Cold Springs subdivision. The 1910 Census lists their nearest neighbors as the twenty-eight children, ages three to sixteen, of St. John's Orphanage, 2403 Linden Avenue. The Queeners lived at their Cold Springs address until at least 1917. That year, the widowed Mrs. Jackson Queener left Elmwood Park and moved out to Cold Springs, taking a house at 2415 Magnolia, across the street from Mr. and Mrs. Washington Queener, perhaps to be near them.

In the meantime, the Queeners' 1886 Victorian at 1702 East Fifth that burned to the ground in 1907 was replaced with a 1909 Colonial by the next owners, the Blacks. Eighty years later, a Bensey family, cousins of the Queeners, bought the 1909 Colonial, where the author currently lives.

Queener, 1520 Magnolia Avenue, Elmwood Park

The family of Andrew Jackson Queener lived in Park City during the 1900s to the 1920s. Known as Jackson Queener, he was born in 1853 in Anderson County, Tennessee, the eighth child and sixth son of Jane Keeney and Grandison Queener and brother of Park City resident George Washington Queener, born in 1854, who also went by his middle name. The brothers were grandsons of Jacob Queener, who came from Germany in the 1700s and settled south of Big Creek Gap, now Jacksboro, in Campbell County, Tennessee.

In 1879, Jackson Queener, twenty-six, and his wife, Martha, twenty, were married and became parents of four children, including Martha, born in 1882; Jessica, born in 1886; and Oliver, born in 1888. Martha married Clease Teagaarden in 1903, when he was eighteen and she was twenty-one, and they had a little girl named Marguerite in 1904. At some point after 1905, the family came to Knox County, following the Washington Queener family, who appeared in the Park City area of Knox County between 1895 and 1900. The Jackson Queener family was living in the Elmwood Park neighborhood of Park City by 1907; that year they had a house at 1613 Bell Avenue, later called Jackson, then McCalla; the next year, they had moved two blocks to the northwest.

From 1908 through 1916, Martha and Jackson Queener lived at 1520 Magnolia Avenue, a circa 1886 Victorian previously inhabited by Juliet Park and Andrew Park White and their daughters, Isabel and Juliet. The Queeners' grown children lived with them; the 1910 census lists Martha Queener Teagarden, twenty-seven; Clease Teagarden, twenty-four; their daughter Marguerite Teagarden, six; Jessica Queener, twenty-three; and Oliver Queener, twenty-one. Also living with the family in 1910 was Jackson Queener's widowed sister Thomasina Queener Perkins, called Sina.

Jackson Queener's brother Washington Queener was living at 1702 East Fifth Avenue, Elmwood Park, a circa 1886 Victorian, where they moved between 1895 and 1900 and stayed until 1907. In 1907, the house burned, and the Washington Queener family moved nine blocks east to 2442 Magnolia Avenue, where they lived until at least 1917. That year, the widowed Mrs. Jackson Queener and her family left Elmwood Park and moved out to Cold Springs, taking a house at 2415 Magnolia, across the street from Mr. and Mrs. Washington Queener, perhaps to be near them.

SELDEN, 1416 LINDEN AVENUE (CHILHOWEE), ELMWOOD PARK

Mr. and Mrs. Andrew K. Selden lived with their family at 1416 Linden Avenue, on the south side near Winona Street in the 1880s–1900s. Mrs. Selden was one of the former Kearsley sisters of Virginia; her two sisters, Mrs. Caldwell and Mrs. Galyon, lived nearby with their families. Andrew Selden and his brother-in-law Thomas Caldwell ran a grocery together on the east side Market Square in downtown Knoxville. Andrew Selden also worked as a contractor, and Thomas Caldwell had also been in business as Shoemaker and Caldwell. The Seldens were not listed in the city directory, but by 1888 they were residing in Elmwood Park, where many new houses were being built in the 1880s. Neighbor and author Lucy Curtis Templeton recalled Selden sons Kenneth and Kearsley and daughter Annie. The 1894 *Knoxville Blue Book* and the 1900 *Knoxville Cookbook* show the Seldons still living at 1416 Linden Avenue. Their street was renamed Chilhowee Avenue in later years.

SHERSKY, 1304 EAST FIFTH AVENUE, ELMWOOD PARK

In 1930, the Shersky family lived at 1304 East Fifth Avenue, Elmwood Park, on the south side of the street, just west of Caswell Park: Robert, forty-two; his wife, Dora, thirty-six; and their children Anna, fifteen; Leonard, fourteen; and Harold, eleven. The house is no longer standing.

By 1955, the Sherskys had moved to other neighborhoods. Dora and Robert Shersky, in their sixties, were living at 101 Magnolia in Old North Knoxville; Harold, thirty-six, and his wife, Adeline, were still in Park City, living at 2438 Linden Avenue, Cold Springs, and Harold's Deli on Gay Street had been open for about a decade.

Stephens, Bell Street, Elmwood Park

Mr. and Mrs. Thomas Stephens made their home on Bell Street at the corner of Howard, now Linden, near First Creek, in one of the older houses in the Elmwood Park subdivision of Shieldstown. Elisabeth Compton, twenty-two, and Thomas Stephens, twenty-six, a carpenter, were married in 1856 and were the parents of at least six children born between 1862 and 1878: John, Caledonia, Charity, Thomas, Francis and James.

Elisabeth Compton was from an old Virginia family transplanted to Tennessee, the eldest of six children born to Sarah Fugate and Henry Compton between 1833 and 1849: Elisabeth, John, Ellen Jane, Virginia, Eliza and William, who died young. The family moved to Grainger County in 1842 and to Knox County in 1853. Their father, Henry Compton, died early in 1854, possibly from a cholera epidemic, leaving behind a widow and five children, ages six through twenty. He is buried in Old Gray Cemetery on Broadway in Knoxville. Elisabeth's widowed mother and youngest sister, Eliza, nine at the time of Elisabeth's marriage, lived with the Stephens family; the 1860 census showed the widowed Sarah Fugate Compton with Eliza, thirteen, as part of the Stephens household on Bell Street.

Thomas Stephens was born in 1829 in England. When the Civil War came to Shieldstown, he became a captain in the Second Tennessee Calvary of the Union army, whose headquarters were in Blount County, Tennessee. Elisabeth's mother and sister continued to live with the Stephens family throughout the war. After the war, in 1866, Eliza Compton, nineteen, married James Wright, twenty, and moved to 100 West Fifth Avenue, North Knoxville.

Sarah Fugate Compton continued to live with her daughter Elisabeth Compton Stephens on Bell Street in Elmwood Park from 1860 until

1886, then with her daughter Eliza and her husband, James Wright, until her death in 1890. Writer Lucy Curtis Templeton described the elderly, widowed "Grandma Compton," as stout and neat, wearing a cap and living "in a cottage of an earlier era," the Stephens house from 1856 or before.

Captain Thomas Stephens, longtime head of the household, died in 1897 of consumption and was buried at the Civil War veterans' National Cemetery in Knoxville. Elisabeth Compton Stephens stayed on in the 1850s house on Bell Street, where she had lived for over fifty years, from her marriage in 1856 until her death in 1908, and was buried at Old Gray Cemetery in Knoxville.

Chapter 10

PRESERVATION EFFORTS

In 1990, the Park City Historic District was placed on the National Register of Historic Places, the federal government's official list of sites and structures deemed worthy of preservation. The Park City Historic District offers guidelines for historic preservation and embraces parts of the historic town: the northern sections of Elmwood Park, Poplar Springs and Cold Springs, but not the southern sections; most of Edgewood and Hazen Hill, though not all; none of East End; and one street of Lake Park Springs. The Park City Historic District is bounded by Washington Avenue on the north, Magnolia Avenue on the south, Cherry Street on the East and First Creek on the west. The district also covers East Fifth Avenue eastward to Chilhowee Park to include the beautiful Lake Park Springs neighborhood.

In 1997, the Edgewood Historic Overlay of the Park City Historic District was established on Washington and Jefferson Avenues, offering greater protection for the structures in the district and stricter guidelines for historic preservation. With its two dozen or more Barber-designed homes preserved much as they were a century ago, this area is a gem of Knoxville and of interest to Barber house enthusiasts nationwide.

The 1854–2004 sesquicentennial of Shieldstown was observed by a few Park City residents and descendants taking an interest in this antebellum village by researching and discussing its history and gathering neighbors to maintain the Shieldstown Cemetery. The year 1854 marked the purchase

A brick pillar survives in the 1500–1600 block on the north side of McCalla Avenue, Elmwood Park. The house is long gone from this once elite neighborhood. *Photo by Margery W. Bensey.*

of land by Shieldstown's founder, and 2004 was a major year for cemetery restoration and historic research. The early Shieldstown residents buried in the cemetery had been documented by cemetery historian Robert McGinnis, whose research was published in his book *Historic Cemeteries of Old Knoxville.* This publication has greatly facilitated the author's research of Shieldstown families, providing addresses and family relationships for some, used in conjunction with Knoxville area city directories and Knox County census records from about 1860 through 1940.

Park City observed its 1907–2007 centennial with rose-colored floral banners on one of its main streets. An eight-page Centennial Edition of an area newsletter, *The Parkridge Press,* was produced, with articles about the founding of the town and life in Park City during that era. A tradition of historic home tours was established in the 1990s and 2000s, offering visitors an opportunity to see inside the houses, with a Centennial Home Tour offered in 2007. A book on Park City was produced on the eve of the centennial, *Images of America: Park City*, and reproductions of George Barber's *Cottage Souvenir No. 2* and *Modern Dwellings* house plans preceded and followed the celebration.

The centennials of the 1910 and 1911 Appalachian Expositions at Chilhowee Park were observed with the 2010 and 2011 Tennessee Valley Agricultural and Industrial Fair those years, and every year, as the fair is an annual occurrence. Events include livestock shows, arts and crafts exhibits, canning contests and amusement park rides.

A statewide and countywide Civil War Sesquicentennial observation throughout 2011–2015 recognizes the 1861–1865 occupations and difficulties of wartime in Shieldstown and the surrounding area, including the demise of the 1854 Octagon House, the burning of all trees in the farmland settlements, the Victorian subdivisions that weathered the storm and the forts on the bluffs above the area that became Park City. The research and recognition of this historic area continues.

BIBLIOGRAPHY

Allen, Ron. *Knoxstalgia*. Knoxville, TN: self-published, 1999.

Ash, Stephen V. *A Year in the South: Four Lives in 1865*. New York: Palgrave McMillan, 2002.

———. *Victorian Cottage Architecture: An American Catalog of Designs*. Mineola, NY: Dover, 2004.

Barber, George W. *Turn-of-the-Century Houses: Elevations and Floor Plans*. Mineola, New York: Dover, 2008.

Bensey, Margery W. "Bensey Genealogies," "Weber Genealogies" and "Shieldstown Genealogies." Unpublished manuscripts, possession of author, Knoxville, Tennessee.

———. "Searching for Shieldstown," "Shieldstown Streets" and "Shieldstown Families." Unpublished manuscripts, possession of author, Knoxville, Tennessee.

———. "A Visit to Blackberry Corner." Unpublished manuscript, possession of author, Knoxville, Tennessee.

———. "The Winter of Blackberry Corner." *HomeWorks: A Book of Tennessee Writers*. Knoxville: University of Tennessee Press, 1996. Reprinted in *Knoxville Christmas 2008*, edited by Cynthia Mobley. Knoxville, TN: Greyhound Press, 2008.

Booker, Robert J. "Keeping Historic Cemetery Clean is Worthy Project." *Knoxville News Sentinel*, October 7, 2003.

———. *Two Hundred Years of Black Culture in Knoxville Tennessee, 1791–1991*. Virginia Beach, VA: Donning, 1993.

Brewer, Becky French, and Douglas Stuart McDaniel. *Images of America: Park City*. Charleston: Arcadia Publishing, 2005.

Davis, William C. *Touched by Fire: A National Historical Society Photographic Portrait of the Civil War*. New York: Black Dog and Leventhal, 1997.

Deaderick, Lucille. *Heart of the Valley: A History of Knoxville, Tennessee*. Knoxville: East Tennessee Historical Society, 1976.

Edgewood-Park City Design Guidelines. Knoxville, TN: Historic Knoxville Zoning Commission, 1997.

Finley, Willis T. "Davis Genealogy." Unpublished manuscript.

Gardner, Christopher. Personal correspondence, 2005.

Hale, Billie Cox, and W. Todd Groce. "Major Benjamin F. Welcker." *Roane County Heritage Book*. Waynesville, NC: Walsworth Publishing, 1999.

Huey, Darlene. Personal correspondence, 2005.

Humes, Thomas W. *The Loyal Mountaineers of Tennessee*. Knoxville, TN: Ogden Brothers and Company,1888.

Hunter, Jeannine F. "Move Underway to Document Underground Railroad in Knoxville." *Knoxville News Sentinel*, February 23, 2001.

Karns, T.C. "The University of Tennessee." In Herbert Baxter Adams, *Contributions to American Educational History*, Vol. 16. Web.

Knoxville Blue Book. Knoxville, Tennessee, 1894.

Knoxville City Directory. Knoxville, Tennessee, 1859–1940.

Knoxville Telephone Directory. Knoxville, Tennessee, 1955.

Manning, Russ, and Sondra Jamieson. *Historic Knoxville and Knox County: A Walking and Touring Guide*. Norris, TN: Laurel Place, 1990.

McDaniel, Douglas Stuart. "Andrew McMillan." *Restore Knoxville*. Knoxville, 2004. Web.

———. *North Knoxville*. Knoxville, TN: Park City Press, 2011.

———. *Oakwood and Lincoln Park*. Knoxville, TN: Park City Press, 2009.

McGinnis, Robert A. *Historic Cemeteries of Old Knoxville*. Knoxville, TN: self-published, 2004.

Mott, Nancy. Personal interview and correspondence, June and July 2012.

Poe, Orlando M., and Cleveland Rockwell. Topographical Map of the Approaches and Defenses of Knoxville, E. Tennessee, Showing the Positions Occupied by the Confederate Forces During the Siege Department of the Ohio, 1863–1864. New York: The Graphic Co., 1864.

———. "The Topography of Knoxville and Its Vicinity." In *The Loyal Mountaineers of Tennessee*, edited by Thomas W. Humes. Knoxville, TN: Ogden Brothers and Company, 1888.

Poole, Rosalyn. Personal interview and correspondence, June and July 2012.

Reeves, Charles A., Jr. "A Map of the Siege of Knoxville, 1863–1864, Showing Streets as They Are Today." Knoxville: Civil War Sesquicentennial Commission of Knox County, 2010.

Rogers, Frank T., ed. *Knoxville Cook Book 1900*. Knoxville, TN: self-published, 1957.

Rothrock, Mary Utopia. *The French Broad-Holston Country: A History of Knox County, Tennessee*. Knoxville, TN: East Tennessee Historical Society, 1946.

Sanford, Edward J. "Narrative." *The Loyal Mountaineers of Tennessee*. Thomas W. Humes, ed. Knoxville, TN: Ogden Brothers and Company, 1888. Web.

Schaich, Helen Pickell. Personal interview, April 2005.

Seymour, Digby G. *Divided Loyalties: Fort Sanders and the Civil War in East Tennessee*. Nashville: East Tennessee Historical Society, 1990.

Smith, Clara Prater. "Benjamin Franklin Welcker." *Roane County Heritage Book*. Waynesville, NC: Walsworth Publishing, 1999.

———. "Dixie Welcker." *Roane County Heritage Book*. Waynesville, NC: Walsworth Publishing, 1999.

———. Personal interview and correspondence, April 2005.

Sutherland, Daniel E., ed. *A Very Violent Rebel: The Civil War Diary of Ellen Renshaw House*. Knoxville: University of Tennessee Press, 1996.

Templeton, Lucy Curtis. "Country Calendar." *Knoxville News Sentinel*, May 10, 1948.

Tumblin, James Connor. "James McMillan." *Fountain City Facts, Myths, and Mysteries*. February 2009. Web.

United States Census, Knox County, Tennessee, 1860–1940.

Welcker, Dixie. 1925 Diary, in the possession of Jim Welcker, quoted by Clara Prater Smith, personal communication, 2005.

Welcker, William Lewis II. "The Descendents of William Lewis Welcker and Malinda Louisa Welcker." Undated typescript in possession of Margery Weber Bensey.

ABOUT THE AUTHOR

Margery (Meg) Weber Bensey is a writer, editor and teacher living in the Park City Historic District of Knoxville, Tennessee. She is a member of Knox Heritage and the Knoxville Civil War Roundtable, as well as the East Tennessee Historical Society. She has been researching the history of her house, its families and Park City since 1989.

Her essays, poems, articles, histories, short stories and illustrations have been published in literary and academic newsletters, four anthologies and a history book. She has a master's degree in literature from the University of Tennessee, where she worked as a writer and editor for twenty years. She is now a writing instructor for local community colleges and a freelance editor.